1970

Becoming a Teacher

The Passage to
Professional Status

ELIZABETH M. EDDY

TEACHERS COLLEGE PRESS

Teachers College, Columbia University

Supported by a grant from the Office of Juvenile Delinquency and
Youth Development, Welfare Administration, Department of Health,
Education and Welfare, Washington, D.C., in cooperation with the
President's Committee on Juvenile Delinquency and Youth Crime.

Manufactured in the United States of America

FOREWORD

Public education in the big cities is in deep trouble. The distress and the disturbances are particularly acute in the inner city. It is here that massed populations of racial and ethnic minorities, with their heavy preponderance of the poor, are beginning to challenge a system, not alone the educational one, which has denied them participation in the decisions which affect their lives. From their perspective the oppression is near universal, and schools are handy targets for venting their hostility.

To say that those who administer the schools are not entirely blameless for the obvious failure to educate the children of the poor is an understatement. Even the most obdurate defenders are now willing to admit that something more can be done—a great concession for those who once rejected all suggestions that evaluation and reform were needed. Less than five years ago the superintendent of America's largest metropolitan school system publicly rebuked his mayor who sought to make changes in school operation, claiming that his school system was the best in the world. Since then bitter conflict has engulfed that system and necessitated direct legislative action to begin the restructuring of a rigid and outmoded enterprise.

It will not be easy to break the hold of vested interests and drag school organization and practices into the twentieth century. It is also obvious that reform cannot be expected to be generated from within; only the demands of an aroused public and revelations demonstrating the inadequacies of present practices will move us to provide the kind of educational experience that all of our children should have. It is because it partially fulfills the latter need that this study by Dr. Elizabeth Eddy achieves such immediate pertinence.

Each year thousands of recently graduated recruits to education enter the classroom for the first time to begin acting out their new role as teachers. Young as they are, they have given a great chunk of their lives in preparation for such a career—informally, from the day they first became registered pupils and formally, through the years spent in teacher-training institutions. Nevertheless, most of those who enter the classrooms of the inner-city schools are woefully unprepared for what they encounter. True enough, they have served a brief internship under the guidance of an experienced teacher, and they are subject to a dull and perfunctory period of orientation before they meet their first classes, an orientation which informs them of their place in a technical and administrative hierarchy. Ultimately, however, it is from the sharp reality of the classroom, sometimes rewarding, sometimes punishing, and of their relationships with their teaching colleagues and those who supervise them that they receive the lasting imprint which shapes their perspective and behavior as teachers.

These are the matters about which Dr. Eddy informs us. She describes and analyzes the experiences of twenty-two beginning teachers during this fateful period of their career. She reveals the pervasive anxieties they suffer and their sometimes frenzied attempts to maintain control. For some few their job becomes a purely custodial one. For a few others the teaching experience fulfills their aspirations. These are the ones who have been claimed by their students and accepted by their peers, and in their acceptance of the bestowal of trust they have become helpers on the path of learning. It is not curious, but sad, that the effects of the administrative presence in this crucial process is almost entirely negative.

As the empirical evidence is unfolded, Dr. Eddy gives us depth of understanding through her utilization of theories of transition derived from the studies of rites of passage by the late French anthropologist Arnold van Gennep. We can learn that the divergent outcomes of the initial period of teaching are due, not to fortuitious or idiosyncratic factors, but to dynamic processes in the school environment.

It is easy to allocate blame for the failures of the past. What is important, however, is whether or not those who train teachers and administer the schools will utilize the knowledge about the educative process which is no accumulating. If they do not or cannot, then it is only too clear that the responsibility of educating should no longer be theirs. This study provides the basis for significant changes in an important area—the teacher training process and the induction of new teachers.

SOLON T. KIMBALL

ACKNOWLEDGEMENTS

This books could not have been written without the weekly tape-recorded reports of twenty-two beginning teachers who, during their first semester of teaching, told of their experiences in schools attended primarily by children of the urban poor in a Northern city. These young men and women must remain anonymous, but the author is deeply indebted to them.

The gathering of the teachers' reports and their subsequent analysis and presentation in book form were sponsored by Project TRUE (Teacher Resources for Urban Education), a curriculum development project undertaken by the Teacher Education Program at Hunter College of the City University of New York. Funds for this project were primarily provided by Training Grants No. 64227 and 65228 from the Office of Juvenile Delinquency and Youth Development, the United States Department of Health, Education and Welfare, in cooperation with the President's Committee on Juvenile Delinquency and Youth Crime.

In addition to the author, the following persons regularly listened to the tapes recorded by one or more teachers each week: Victor Balaban, Robert F. Beauchamp, Estelle Fuchs, Paul Lamb, Katherine McKinnon, Sandra E. Motz, Helen Randolph, Robert H. Roth, Helen F. Storen, Andre L. Thibodeau, Elaine Waldman, Nancy O'Brien Scheuler, and Marjorie B. Smiley. As indicated in the text, these persons provided personal responses to each teacher's weekly report through letters to the teacher or teachers to whom they were assigned.

The development of the questions to be asked of each teacher was primarily the responsibility of the author but was greatly aided by the suggestions of Marjorie B. Smiley and Harry L. Miller. Estelle Fuchs revised the questions asked of elementary-school teachers so that they would be appropriate for junior-high-school teachers.

The work of developing a code for the recorded material and then coding the transcripts was undertaken by the author, Edwin Chin-Shong, Helen Randolph, and George Yonemura. The burden of abstracting coded materials fell upon Helen Randolph, who was aided in this task by Carol Bryant and Helene R. Siegel. Susanne Landfield carefully summarized the material which provides the basis for Chapters 3 and 4.

The transcription of the tapes and the typing of the several drafts of the manuscript was the work of Masako Mae Kanazawa, Elaine Paul, Jeanne Randolph, and Nancy Stevenson. Norman Bailey and Susan J. Strausberg provided administrative assistance which facilitated the preparation of the book.

Finally, the book has been greatly enriched by discussion with colleagues at Hunter College and the University of Florida. Among these, Marjorie B. Smiley and Solon T. Kimball provided special help by reading and commenting on early drafts.

Although all of the above persons and institutions have contributed to the book in many ways, sole responsibility for the viewpoints expressed in the following pages rests with the author.

E.M.E.

CONTENTS

INTRODUCTION

Teachers in urban slum areas have traditionally been the bearers of the cultural skills and knowledge which have enabled many generations of urban poor to rise to higher social positions in our society. For the past decade, however, teachers in these schools have been increasingly under fire because of their inability to educate the child of the contemporary slum and to provide him with the necessary training for success in school and eventual incorporation into a modern technological society. Whereas teachers are commonly credited with having successfully educated the children of foreign immigrant groups, their record with the children of rural Americans who have migrated to the cities in search of employment is viewed as one of dismal failure. The problem has become so serious that it has attracted widespread public attention and led to boycotts, demands of Negro parents for greater control of the schools their children attend, and such popular books as *The Blackboard Jungle, To Sir, With Love, Up the Down Staircase, The Schoolchildren, Our Children Are Dying, Death at an Early Age, 36 Children,* and *Dead End School.* [1]

In response, educators and other community leaders are examin-

[1] Evan Hunter, *The Blackboard Jungle* (New York: Simon and Schuster, 1954); Edward R. Braithwaite, *To Sir, With Love* (Englewood Cliffs, N. J.: Prentice-Hall, 1960); Bel Kaufman, *Up the Down Staircase* (Englewood Cliffs, N. J.: Prentice-Hall, 1964); Mary Frances Greene and Orletta Ryan, *The Schoolchildren: Growing Up in the Slums* (New York: Pantheon Books, 1965); Nat Hentoff, *Our Children Are Dying* (New York: Viking Press, 1966); Jonathan Kozol, *Death at an Early Age* (Boston: Houghton Mifflin Company, 1967); Herbert Kohl, *36 Children* (New York: New American Library, 1967) ; Robert Coles, *Dead End School* (Boston: Little, Brown and Company, 1968).

1

ing new approaches in the formal training of teachers who will
work in the modern urban slum.[2] Since the early 1960's, urban
affairs and problems have received growing attention. Conferences,
books, articles, and speeches have emphasized the need for better
education of the poor, and several proposals have been made for
recruiting and training persons to teach in urban slums. Until now,
the discussion and remedial proposals have often been centered on
the negative attributes of teachers and their pupils which make it
difficult for the two groups to engage successfully in educational
work, and on the contrasting positive attributes of teachers and the
educational techniques which might improve the present situation.[3] Emphasis has been placed on the "middle-class" teacher and
the "lower-class" child, and on the necessity of bridging the cultural gap between the two.

Important as this approach to our understanding of the current
situation may be, it does not pay sufficient attention to the social
context within which teachers and pupils encounter one another.
The teacher-pupil relationship is only one of many relationships in
the formal educational institution. School administrators, specialists,
and other personnel all make substantial contributions to the social
context within which the traits of both teachers and students
become defined and find meaning. The teacher's classroom may be
his castle, but in the contemporary school the classroom is an inte-
gral part of the surrounding educational system. To concentrate
upon only the attributes of teachers and pupils is to ignore significant dimensions which affect the outcome of the educational effort.

Although this book concerns the problem of teacher preparation
and recruitment for the school in the slum, the goal is not to provide a catalogue of "good" or "bad" traits which, if added or sub-
tracted, would produce better teachers. Rather, the central theme
is the relationship between teacher performance in the school and
the official as well as covert socialization of beginning teachers by
those who have preceded them. The experiences of beginning
teachers provide a particularly salient source of material germane to
this topic.

The chapters that follow make extensive illustrative use of data

[2]For example, the *Report of the National Advisory Commission on Civil Disorders*
(New York: Bantam Books, 1968) underscores the need for "a national effort to
attract to the teaching profession well-qualified and highly motivated young people and to equip them to work more effectively with disadvantaged students."

[3]For a recent example of this approach, see Michael Usdan and Frederick Bertolaet,
*Teachers for the Disadvantaged: The Report of the School-University Teacher Edu-
cation Project* (Chicago: Follett Publishing Company, 1966).

gathered in the fall of 1963 and of 1964 from a total of twenty-two teachers whose first formal teaching experience was in a school in a slum area. As background for what follows, significant details of the data collection and important facts about the participants will be presented here.

The group comprised thirteen elementary and nine junior-high-school teachers. They reported their experiences as beginning teachers in the schools of a large northern city on tape recorders during the first semester of teaching. Each week they returned to the publicly-supported, non-residential college from which they had all graduated the previous June. There they responded to a series of questions concerning the most important thing that had happened to them during the week, their least and most successful lessons, their most difficult children, and their interaction with school administrators, specialists, and other teachers. From time to time, questions were asked about other aspects of their experiences, including the general characteristics of their schools and the classes they taught, the textbooks and supplies they used, the meetings they attended, the parents with whom they had contact, their least difficult children, and the informal cliques of teachers to which they belonged. Their attitudes toward and knowledge of special outside events such as threatened teachers' strikes and civil rights boycotts of the schools were also elicited.[4]

These twenty-two teachers were selected from official lists of all June graduates of the college who were starting their teaching careers in schools in the slum areas of the city where the college was also located. The schools in which they taught enrolled an unusually high number of Negro and Puerto Rican students who were behind in educational achievement according to official records of the local Board of Education. In most cases, a majority of the pupils taught by the teachers had parents who were on welfare. All the teachers were assigned to classes designated for "slow" children, although some of the junior-high-school teachers taught one or more subject classes composed of "average" or "bright" children.[5] Four of the junior-high-school teachers taught "out of license," rather than teaching the subjects for which they had been formally prepared and temporarily licensed to teach. The teachers were widely dispersed, in ten elementary schools and seven junior-high schools. Three elementary and two junior-high schools received two teach-

[4]See Appendix A for a listing of the questions asked and further details about data collection.

[5]See Appendix B for a description of the classes taught by each teacher.

ers each from the selected group, while the twelve other schools received only one.

Several differences among the schools are noteworthy. The smallest elementary school had an enrollment of approximately 540 pupils, and the largest had 1500 pupils. The size of the junior-high schools ranged from 1000 to 1900 pupils. All of the elementary schools included kindergarten through the sixth grade. The junior-high schools typically served pupils in the seventh through the ninth grades, but one of them had no ninth grade, one included sixth-grade classes, and one was a school for kindergarten through ninth grade. This last school was located in a white neighborhood, and the majority of the students were white rather than Negro and Puerto Rican. However, Negro and Puerto Rican parents living in other areas could send their children to this school if they made special arrangements with the Board of Education, and a number of them did so. The teacher reporting from this school had some classes primarily attended by such children.[6]

For reporting their experiences, the teachers were paid a salary equivalent to half a day of substitute teaching. Participation was of course voluntary. Efforts to select the teachers on a random basis were made, but other demands on their time prohibited many from participating. As a consequence the final group was selected on the basis of availability for the half day of reporting each week. A brief statement of the background and other characteristics of the twenty-two teachers who agreed to serve as reporters will increase the understanding of their experiences.

The selected teachers were urban in origin, with strong family and educational ties to the local city. With one exception, they had graduated from either public or parochial elementary and secondary schools in the same city as the college from which they had graduated and the schools in which they were teaching. Seventeen of the teachers were single. Of these, sixteen were living at home with their parents.

Many of the teachers were in the process of making social transitions in addition to the one of assuming an adult work role. For example, one of the single teachers was living alone away from home, and eight of the single teachers were engaged to be married at the time they began to teach or became engaged during the first semester of teaching. Five of the teachers were already married when they took their first teaching position, and living in their own homes away from parents. Only one of them diverged from the

[6]The characteristics of each school are given in Appendix C.

others in any measure. She had received extensive schooling outside of the local city, coming to the college attended by the others only to complete work for a degree which had been started elsewhere. Unlike the other teachers who were all in their early twenties, she was in her mid-twenties, and she had a child.

The majority of the teachers had exceeded the educational and occupational achievement of their parents. Data on parental background were available for twenty-one teachers. Of these, all had been born in the United States, and both parents of fourteen of them were also native-born. In only two cases were both parents immigrants. Five of the teachers' fathers had not completed high school; seven had finished high school only; nine had attended college, but only four of these were college graduates. The sixteen fathers who were living were employed in occupations ranging from semiskilled work to lesser management and professional roles. Fourteen of the teachers' mothers were employed, and the total family income ranged from three thousand dollars to over fifteen thousand dollars, with the median income in the eight to nine thousand dollar bracket. Three teachers had one parent employed in the local educational system; their positions were school custodian, school crossing guard, and teacher.[7]

In addition to the above socio-economic characteristics, it may be noted that twenty of the teachers were female. Two of the junior-high-school teachers were male. Only one of the teachers was Negro, the remainder being white. Fourteen of the teachers were Jewish; five were Catholic, and two were Protestant.

The educational background of all of the teachers was similar. All of them had received a bachelor of arts degree. As undergraduates, six had majored in English; three each in history, sociology, and psychology; two in Spanish; and one each in anthropology, political science, and music. The majors of two teachers are unknown. During their college years, all of them had completed a series of professional courses in education and a period of supervised student teaching which had prepared them for provisional state licensing as teachers.

The records of final student teaching grades were available for twenty, all of whom had been given a high rating by the teacher education program which had prepared them. Thirteen had received a grade of A and seven a grade of B. In addition, all of the teachers were "endorsed with confidence" or "enthusiasm" by

[7]A summary of each teacher's socio-economic characteristics is given in Appendix D.

their college supervisors on the characteristics of responsibility, personal and social adjustment, personal appearance, and professional promise. The speech of three teachers was "endorsed moderately," as was the written English of one. The remainder received high endorsement of their speech and writing.

The twenty-two teachers received their first formal teaching appointments in a variety of ways. Although all of them were officially assigned by the local Board of Education, for the majority their appointment to a particular school where they had done student or substitute teaching had been requested by principals who thought well of their work. Nine of the elementary teachers and seven of the junior-high-school teachers received appointments in this fashion. In the case of three elementary-school teachers, prior contact with the school was limited to a few days' substitute teaching during the previous spring. Six other elementary-school teachers had done student teaching in the school to which they were later assigned, and two of these had also done substitute teaching there, and one had attended the school in the first grade. Six of the junior-high-school teachers did student teaching in the schools to which they were appointed as beginning teachers, and two of these were graduates of the same schools. The seventh junior-high-school teacher was also a graduate of the school in which she taught, but her student teaching had been done elsewhere.

A minority of the teachers had no formal contacts with their schools prior to going there to teach. Three of the elementary teachers, however, had informal contacts and were recommended by friends for openings in the schools. Only one of the elementary teachers and two of the junior-high teachers received their first teaching appointment without having had any previous contact with anyone in the school. Two were simply assigned by the local Board of Education. The third responded to a newspaper ad and went for an interview with the principal, who then requested that she be assigned to his school.

The experiences of these beginning teachers, and others with similar characteristics who begin their teaching careers in similar schools, are the primary subject of this book. Using an anthropological perspective to be described later, new teachers will be viewed as those in the process of making a transition from the status of pupil to that of teacher. This is not an easy transition in any case, but it is especially difficult in the school in the slum area because the newcomer often encounters unfamiliar behavior on the part of pupils and sometimes on the part of others in the school. Yet here, as in other schools, new teachers find those who try to reach out and help them through what all agree is a difficult year.

In presenting the reports of one group of teachers about their experiences with those who preceded them in the school and attempted to socialize them for their teaching roles in the slum, the intent is not to provide the reader with generalizations about all beginning teachers in all schools everywhere. Rather, the purpose is to provide a greater understanding of the social relationships within the school which deeply affect new teachers and their teaching performance and which must be taken into account if teacher education and recruitment is to become more meaningful for those who teach in slum areas. This book is directed toward this problem, and the problem is one which even this limited sample of teachers describes eloquently.

1

TEACHERS IN TRANSITION

Each fall thousands of those who once were students become teachers. With their recently acquired certificates of graduation, they enter the classroom in a new position, as those who stand in front of students and direct their activities. These young men and women, equipped with chalk, class records, seating charts, and teaching manuals, are at the starting point of their career. For some, the return to school is an educational homecoming to schools and communities in which they grew up. For others, it is an educational departure as they enter schools far away from family and friends. For all, the moment of re-entry into the educational system is filled with hopes and expectations but also fraught with qualms and anxiety about their new role.

The first year of teaching is a hard one. Gone are the days of talking freely with students as peers and joining their discussions about teachers. No longer students but teachers in charge, the newcomers feel the difference and wonder if they can cope with the task ahead. The weight of their new responsibility is heavy. Much must be learned about teaching, the school, the children. The fatigue at the end of the day is incredible. The paperwork is overwhelming. Uncertainty about the ability to establish authority in the classroom makes them tense. The classroom, once so familiar, has new and different dimensions when one must stand in front and face the pupils.

On the surface, it is strange that beginning to teach should be so difficult. The educational system recruits as teachers those who have spent many years as pupils within its ranks. New teachers have usually spent most of their lives in schools not too dissimilar from those in which they begin their careers. First, there have been the elementary, intermediate, and high-school years, the selection of the academic classes and the preparation for college. More recently, there have been the college years, the decision to teach, and the formal training in the specialized courses specifically designed to prepare students to remain within the educational system rather than leave it, as will their peers who pursue other occupations. In contrast to trainees for other types of work, who never, or for very limited periods, have a chance to observe experienced workers, those preparing to teach have watched experienced teachers for years and have subtly learned a good deal about what it is that teachers do and how they do it. Even if the student days of observing teachers have resulted in only unconscious learning, there has been the period of formal preparation, including especially the student teaching experience, which is deliberately intended to enable students to make the transition to the role of teacher. Why then should the first year of teaching in any school be the ordeal that it frequently is, and why is it especially difficult in those schools serving the contemporary urban poor?

To answer this question, it is necessary to consider the primary emphasis of the socialization which new teachers have received during their many years as pupils and students, the limitations of past experience as a guideline for the teacher's present conduct, the dissimilarities between the roles of student teacher and actual teacher, and the significant aspects of making a social transition from one position to another in a society. This chapter gives attention to these matters as a prelude to the subsequent chapters, which will be concerned with the socialization of teachers into their new work once they have formally become members of the teaching staff.

THE YEARS OF PARTICIPANT OBSERVATION

Like all roles in society, those of pupil and teacher are ones which must be learned. Essentially, the role of pupil requires behavior appropriate to a subordinate position and a prolonged period of continued dependency on adults in the school. The many years of formal schooling emphasize this dependency and the cultural contrast between the pupil who must obey and the adult who commands. As former pupils, teachers have been conditioned to be submissive doers of the schoolwork initiated by adult teachers. Their learning has been primarily oriented toward the mastery of subject matter and becoming socialized into the student body.

It is true that most new teachers are in the same general type of school environment that they were in as pupils. Now, however, they have a superordinate role which requires that they socialize pupils for subordinate roles. Little in their past experience prepares them for this task, and even the months of student teaching can only partially bridge the gap separating the role of adult as teacher from child as pupil.[1]

Abrupt changes in relationships with others mark the transition from pupil to teacher. These changes are succinctly evident in the fact that while teachers are now formally addressed by students, they have the privilege of calling students by their first names and are at last on a first-name basis with other teachers. Then too, there are the shifts from being the questioned to being the questioner, from being the one who does the work assigned by others to being the one who tells others what to do. Yet teachers quickly discover that there is nothing magical in their new position which automatically insures the desired performance from the children. Authority in the classroom is not conferred together with the provisional license to teach. It must be forged out of human relationships with the class and awarded by pupils themselves.[2] Only the children can truly validate the professional role by doing their lessons and learning the knowledge and skills taught, thereby claiming the professional work as worthwhile.

As college graduates, new teachers have achieved success in the educational system. They have spent their time as pupils largely in the company of peers who have also done schoolwork well. They have fulfilled many, if not all, of their own teachers' expectations. Thus they bring to their new positions specific expectations about the nature of the school and the types of human activities and relationships which are appropriate in the classroom. They may

[1] Ruth Benedict has noted that dominance-submission, "where like does not respond to like, but where one type of behavior stimulates the opposite response," is one of the most prominent ways in which behavior is patterned in American culture. It is one of the central cultural themes which the school transmits to the child. See Ruth Benedict, "Continuities and Discontinuities in Cultural Conditioning," in Clyde Kluckhohn and Henry A. Murray, eds., *Personality in Nature, Society, and Culture* (New York: Alfred A. Knopf, 1948), pp. 414–423.

[2] See Chester I. Barnard, "A Definition of Authority," in Robert K. Merton, Ailsa P. Gray, Barbara Hockey, Hanan C. Selvin, eds., *Reader in Bureaucracy* (Glencoe, Ill.: The Free Press, 1952): "If a directive communication is accepted by one to whom it is addressed, its authority for him is confirmed or established. It is admitted as the basis of action. Disobedience of such a communication is a denial of its authority for him. Therefore, under this definition the decision as to whether an order has authority or not lies with the persons to whom it is addressed, and does not reside in 'persons of authority' or those who issue these orders" (p.180).

experience a feeling of shock when they meet pupils in the school who do not share their expectations.

In the school in the urban slum, beginning teachers are especially apt to find children who are unlike what they remember themselves as being when they were school children. For these teachers the contrast between what they themselves experienced over a long period and what they encounter in teaching their first classes is particularly sharp, and they quickly recognize that the situation is not one with which they are familiar:[3]

The most important feeling that I had this week was that Open School Week in this school was very different than it was when I was a child and went to school. When I was younger and we had Open School Week, every single parent came. The room was just filled with parents, and so naturally I expected the same thing. I didn't even think twice about it. I had prepared the children for this. . . . Only four parents came. . . . My feelings when this happened were just to sort of give me another shock and make me a little more aware of how different the environment of these children is from the environment that I and my friends grew up in and went to public school in. I am continually being reminded of this, and this was just one more thing to remind me of it.

*   *   *   *   *

In general, I am appalled and can't even conceive of the actions that these kids participate in and the language that they use. I have to remind myself that I have a very different background from theirs, but I keep putting myself in their place. I keep remembering when I was in school, how I wanted to learn, how I was respectful—not that I was a perfect angel, because I wasn't, but I had very good marks, and I received many awards at the end of the junior-high-school career, and I also made the opening speech at graduation. I just can't conceive of how these kids are forever screaming and fighting. . . . This utter lack of respect and the slamming of doors, using filthy words, telling me to drop dead is really the thing that shocked me these past few months. . . .

The assistant principal told me that the school was much better now than when I was there. He meant this with respect to reading and math grades. I disagree with him. Just going through the yearbook, you can see such a vast difference. When I was in the school, there was no such thing as corrective reading. Most of the kids were reading on grade, and we didn't have such problem classes as we do now.

[3]The twenty-two teachers were not specifically questioned on this point; however, in response to other questions, the effects of the past days as a student were spontaneously mentioned. All quotations from teachers used in this and later chapters are taken from the reports of the twenty-two teachers and have been edited to preserve the anonymity of all schools and persons.

The influence of the past years as pupils in the school is not limited to the acquisition of expectations about the way pupils and parents should respond to the educational effort. Training in techniques of classroom management and teaching also takes place as the pupils observe their teachers:

The tearing up of exams is an old trick I learned when I was in the eighth grade. I remember I had a teacher who had given us twenty adjectives to memorize. We were then supposed to list them and write a sentence for each one. I was in a good class. It was a bright class. As in all classes, we all had our days, and we were a bit noisy. I remember the teacher administered the test, and still there was some muttering and grumbling going on. He calmly took the pack of papers, and he tore them up and stacked them in the ash can. He then looked at us and said, "We're going to take the test again, and if you insist on being noisy, I will tear up the papers again, and we will continue doing this until you are absolutely silent." Needless to say, we got the message, and we were very quiet. . . .

The first time I did this was on the first test that I gave all my classes this term. In practically all my math classes, I had to tear up one or two papers just to make the kids realize I meant business. This was mostly for the kids that were noisy or who kept annoying others.

*   *   *   *   *

There is one thing I want to stress with them. This is seeing relationships between numbers, which is something I never learned when I was in elementary school, and it always seemed to make math very dull for me. And I remember taking a course in high school where the teacher began at the beginning of the term by doing some very elementary things. He talked about ten and what ten is, and he really made us see what numbers are and what they do. . . . I want to convey some of this to my class.

The examples cited highlight only a few of the things that teachers learn about school while they attend school. They serve to emphasize the basic point that the training of teachers for their formal role begins long before courses in education are taken. For all teachers the prolonged socialization into a dependency role is apt to make the transition into a superordinate role difficult. For beginning teachers in schools in slum or other areas in which pupils are socially and culturally different from those they have known, the educational expectations and techniques acquired during this early training are likely to be inappropriate for large numbers of the children they must now teach.

TRAINING FOR SEPARATION FROM THE STUDENT ROLE

There is not only the failure of the days of pupil observation and experience to bridge the gap between the child-pupil and the adult-teacher. There is also the failure of the education courses and the student teaching experience to adequately prepare teachers for their new positions in the classroom. While this problem is not confined to teachers who begin their careers in slum areas, it is especially acute there, and much attention is now being given to special training of teachers for the children of the urban poor.

In our large cities, the newcomers to the teaching profession have often been most recently taught by those who have themselves attended the local city schools and are capping long and successful careers in the local educational system by teaching those who will succeed them on the lower rungs of the educational hierarchy. Frequently they "have come up the hard way" and are those for whom education has been a means of upward social mobility and who have a deep sense of loyalty to the local public school system. At the same time, they may also be those for whom extended ties of family and ethnic affiliation are highly important, and they may be strongly local in experience and outlook. The way the local school system is operated may be and frequently is upheld as the only known and best way to do things.[4]

Local educational folklore and tradition is passed from one generation to the next, and the local school system becomes one to be guarded against invasion by outsiders though improvement may be sought from trusted insiders. This type of localism is represented in the extreme by the teachers who, after attending a local metropolitan college, begin their teaching career in a school from which they graduated and in which they did their student teaching. An urban school system dominated by those who have literally never left the local schools and who provide the new teacher with careful training in local traditions and practices which have been successful for them is often seriously out of touch with the special needs of the new generation of children in contemporary schools, especially in slum areas. As a consequence, teachers in training may learn con-

[4]The degree of localism that may pervade an urban school system is well illustrated by the New York City schools. A recent report indicates that perhaps as many as 90 per cent of this system's teachers are graduates of colleges or universities located in the New York City area. Sixty per cent of the teachers are graduates of the City University. "For all intents and purposes, all of the promotional ranks in the system are filled by people who began as teachers in the system and who have moved up the ladder" (Mayor's Advisory Panel on Decentralization of the New York City Schools, *Reconnection for Learning* [New York, 1967], p. 45).

siderably more about the perpetuation of educational techniques that have been successful in the past than they do about the innovative techniques needed if present problems are to be resolved.

The formal socialization provided by courses in education is culminated by student teaching, which is intended to facilitate the transition of students from those who think and act like students to those who think and act like teachers. Student teaching is a cooperative venture between the teacher training institution and conveniently located school systems. The students are placed in a particular school or schools on a full- or part-time basis for a period of several months. In the school, they work under the direction of one or more cooperating teachers, with occasional supervisory visits from a faculty member in the training institution.

During this transitional period of student teaching, the students observe and act out the behaviors they are eventually to assume as teachers. Clerical work, lesson planning, practice teaching, classroom management, and other tasks which teachers perform are assigned to them in varying degrees. The students are observed while teaching, evaluations of them are recorded, and suggestions for improvement of teaching techniques are given to them in supervisory conferences. The students nearly always do well enough that the teacher training institution officially states that they are prepared to teach and declares them deserving of a new status in the educational system.

The circumstances under which student teaching eases the transition from the role of student to that of teacher, and the extent to which it does so, are not empirically known. Yet it seems clear that important learnings about the role of teacher do occur during student teaching and that this time may be particularly useful for the transmission of written and oral traditions about teaching from one generation of teachers to the next. As the following examples indicate, the handing down of written materials, teaching techniques, and classroom management procedures provides a means for the communication of the traditions, beliefs, and customs of the more experienced teachers in the school.

I had Mrs. LaSalle as a cooperating teacher when I student taught in the school, and she gave me a copy of her plan book, and I've been using this as a guide. It just happens to be a very good plan book, and she happens to be an excellent teacher, so I have talked with her, and I'm copying her style of doing it.

        *   *   *   *   *

I'm using this method of teaching reading now because when I student taught it was the method the teacher was using, and naturally because I don't know any other really. You know, you copy their methods because you're there to learn from these teachers and it worked well with her.

＊   ＊   ＊   ＊   ＊

Last year when I student taught, the teacher gave me a whole bunch of rexographs that she had used, and I took them home. I've been using some of them.

＊   ＊   ＊   ＊   ＊

It's from the school that I developed my methods of teaching—from the student teaching. I watched how the other teachers did it, and the assistant principal told me how she wanted it done.

＊   ＊   ＊   ＊   ＊

It is very important for a teacher to always be on her guard and to be very, very strict the first weeks of school. This is something which many people will tell a young teacher, or this is something that we have heard constantly while we were student teaching. This is not to smile for the whole first month of school, not even to smile at all, not to let them get away with anything, and to hold on very tight. Only after you have the children disciplined can you begin to let go. . . .

＊   ＊   ＊   ＊   ＊

There is one thing I learned about a slow class from my student teaching experience. You absolutely cannot teach a slow class anything until you have complete control of that class. I saw my cooperating teacher take period after period just to tell her class and yell at them that they should be quiet, and that they should really obey the rules of the school. This lecturing really did pay off because the class knew she meant business, and she followed up everything she said, and they worked for her.

＊   ＊   ＊   ＊   ＊

I learned from my cooperating teacher that it's a good idea to have everything removed from the desks, because this way they can concentrate on you. If there are any notebooks or papers or pens and pencils, they tend to start playing with them. This way they have nothing to do but keep their hands on their lap or on their desks and look at you.

For those teachers whose first job is in the school where they did student teaching, the student teaching experience provides direct acquaintance with the staff, administrative procedures, and some of the children. Therefore, these teachers presumably have different types of interaction with administrators, peers, and pupils than do those who eventually teach in schools where they have not done student teaching. The evidence is not clear on this point, but the following comments suggest that there are important consequences of returning to a school in which one is already known.

I am quite fortunate in that I student taught in this school last term, and the assistant principal set me up in my room and gave me as many supplies as I thought I needed. . . . He also had me get all my textbooks last year, so that when the children came in I had something to work with.

*   *   *   *   *

I had lunch one day this week with the teacher with whom I student taught last year. She is the teacher to whom I would go if I really had a bad problem. She gives me a lot of helpful hints. For instance, I told her that my children were having trouble recognizing the letters of the alphabet, and she told me the best way to do this was to play a game with them, and the game that we would play would be this. . . . She told me a way to approach the problem I was having with mathematics. . . . She constantly asks me how everything is going. Do I have any problem I want to discuss with her? This week I didn't have anything I wanted to discuss with her, but it made me feel very secure that I have her. She's a wonderful person, and she'll help me with anything at any time.

*   *   *   *   *

She was my cooperating teacher. We are quite close and friendly. If there are any problems I go to her, and she is sort of taking a protective attitude towards me. I find that she has taken my part in several instances when the administration has gotten a little too demanding.

*   *   *   *   *

The man who was my cooperating teacher last term has been a tremendous help this week. He explained all the little details such as attendance books and how attendance cards are made up.

*   *   *   *   *

I student taught in this school, and the minute the UFT chairman in my school found out that I had been appointed to this school, she approached me and asked me if I would like to join and, of course, I joined the group.

*   *   *   *   *

Since I student taught in the school, the administration felt that I knew much about the school, and so they didn't come to me and give me the help which I did need. However, the principal came around to my class the first day. . . and told them that I was a very good teacher, mainly because I had been trained to teach in their school.

The suggestion has frequently been made that teachers be assigned to the school in which they did student teaching, or a similar school, as a means of improving teacher performance in slum areas. On the assumption that student teaching in a school composed of "middle-class" children does not prepare the teacher to teach children from the slums, new experimental programs in teacher education emphasize the importance of deliberately arranging student teaching in slum area schools for those whose first teaching assignment will be there. In some programs there are special arrangements with the Board of Education so that this may be done.[5] These programs have yet to be carefully evaluated. However, the preceding comments indicate that the benefits to future teachers include more than the official rationale that they have a better understanding of and rapport with the pupils. Indeed, it is likely that the primary benefits may have more to do with readily establishing or continuing working relationships with colleagues and administrators to whom one is already known than with teaching pupils more successfully.

Yet it is evident from some of the observations of beginning teachers that student teaching in a school in the slum does not necessarily result in a smooth transition to the teaching role. Although the typical school in these areas is composed primarily of children who are classified as "slow" and "behind" in school work, there are nearly always some classes attended by children who are "average" or above in their abilities. Some student teachers encounter primarily these children and are unaware of the problems presented by the "slow" child until they are assigned their first classes as beginning teachers:

I see a vast difference between student teaching and actual teaching. During student teaching, you're under the watchful supervision of a trained teacher. The classes realize they're rather special and act accordingly. . . . Last year I had the academically top eighth-grade class. . . . I remember eagerly awaiting each day when I was student teaching. . . . Now I look forward to certain classes, lunch, and prep periods. I pray that my "time" with the bottom seventh-grade class goes by real quickly.

       *   *   *   *   *

When I student taught, I taught the average first grade, in which the children really learned things. My second-grade class can't do what this first grade did, and I am assuming they can do it. I just have to start from the beginning and forget that they ever learned anything and just try to build up from the first grade through the second grade. Especially since I have non-readers in the class, I have to start at the beginning.

[5]For a description of one of these programs, see Vernon F. Haubrich, "Teachers for Big-City Schools," in A. Harry Passow, ed., *Education in Depressed Areas* (New York: Teachers College Press, 1963), pp. 243–261.

Because student teaching is invariably done in classes on the grade level and in subject areas the teacher is later licensed to teach, actual assignment to other grades or subjects may be another source of discontinuity between the student teaching experience and the reality of the first teaching assignment, particularly at the junior- and senior-high-school level. The problem is well-stated by a junior-high-school teacher who returned to a school which she had attended and in which she did student teaching:

> I am a social studies major and having to teach math is something that I didn't look forward to. I must admit that I have always hated math. . . I've always been very weak in math, and, as a matter of fact, in high school I flunked every math course I took. . . . When I covered the education sequence in college, I never covered any mathematical subject. . . I never expected to have to teach it.

The dissimilarity between the student teaching and actual teaching experiences entails not only potential differences between schools, grades, and pupils. There are also differences in the responsibility for and relationships with pupils. Student teachers are quite literally neither students nor teachers but persons in the social position of transition, and new teachers are keenly aware of the fact:

> There is a great difference between being a teacher and a student teacher. First of all, when you're a teacher, you have your class for yourself. You start from the beginning in September. These children are all strangers to you. You're a stranger to them. You start on an even basis, and what you build up from there is built between you and your class. When a stranger, which is what a student teacher is, gets up and teaches a lesson, this rapport that the teacher has built up with her class all year long is not there, and the students will react the way they've always reacted to strangers. . . . I always felt when I got up to teach a lesson when I was a student teacher that these children in front of me were strangers, and each lesson was in isolation. As a teacher I feel that I have control, and I care about what they do, how they act in my classroom and with other teachers in other classrooms. This makes my job much more meaningful for me, because I have a set of children that I'm responsible for and that I do care about. . . . This is a feeling a student teacher can never have, because the children do not belong to the student teacher. They belong to the teacher. The teacher starts out with them in September and ends up with them in June. A student teacher is a stranger and will always be a stranger to these pupils.

> *   *   *   *   *

The greatest difference between being a teacher and a student teacher is that the amount of responsibility is tremendous. You are certainly given more power, and you're more involved. You no longer are an onlooker, and you miss some of the observations that you get when you just have time to sit in the back of the room looking and watching students. You don't get this any more when you are standing in front of the room. You no longer see what goes on in the back of the room, and you don't see the students from the back. You see them from the front. You don't see them as each individual responding. You see them as one of a group responding. . . . Your conduct is also a little different. You've got to be a little more reserved. You can't be as friendly with some of the students as you may have been when you were a student teacher. You lose some contact with them. When you are a student teacher, students may talk to you a little more freely or discuss the teacher with whom you are working more freely than they do now when you are the teacher. There is a big difference there. You're the teacher in charge now, and you no longer are just an onlooker and maybe one of them in a way.

Upon the completion of the student teaching experience and the formally prescribed course work, the student is publicly declared by the teacher training institution to be prepared to teach. The formal graduation ceremony and the awarding of the college degree symbolically express the end of the student role and the beginning of a new role. These "strangers" and "outsiders" now have to be incorporated into their new role as teachers. They have observed and learned much about teaching during the long transitional years as students, yet it remains to be fully accepted as teachers by those in the schools to which they will go.

When the summer vacation is over and the fall brings the traditional opening of school, these young men and women will struggle hard for social and personal identity in their new positions. Their success in achieving this identity will depend largely upon those who greet them in the school and attempt to incorporate them into their professional roles. Administrators, fellow teachers, pupils, and others will all play a part in the humdrum activities of the first year of teaching, which, no matter how tedious or difficult, will provide the means for incorporation or rejection of the newcomers.

Many of those who begin teaching in slum areas will encounter special problems due to their orientation toward norms of scholastic achievement, academic progress, and pupil behavior; for such norms are often incongruent with the needs of pupils who are still in the process of urbanization and are unfamiliar or unable to cope with the demands of the school as they are currently presented.[6]

[6]A description of some of the problems presented to school pupils by the present organizational structure of schools in slum areas is presented in Elizabeth M.

Moreover, the professional training of beginning teachers has usually prepared them to teach pupils who respond to the formal education system sufficiently well to do at least average work and to behave in ways acceptable to the school; but it has seldom prepared them to teach pupils who have a history of school failure or underachievement and, in some instances, of disruptive classroom behavior. As a consequence, the successful transition of teachers in these schools is especially difficult and may be pathologic when it does occur.[7] To better understand what is involved and to provide the theoretical background for subsequent chapters, it is necessary now to turn to a general consideration of what it means to be in a process of social transition.

THE SIGNIFICANCE OF SOCIAL TRANSITION

It has been noted that as new teachers complete their formal training and embark upon their professional careers they make a transition from child-pupil to adult-teacher within the educational system. Important changes in relationships to others, status, activities, and procedures accompany this transition. From the subordinate position of pupils who are dependent on teachers, the beginning teachers must move into the superordinate position of those who plan the work that pupils do and socialize them into their dependent roles in the school. The appropriate relationship with teachers is now that of a colleague and peer, although they still maintain a subordinate relationship to school administrators.

New teachers are not unique in experiencing social transition. All individuals experience changes in status and relationships to others in their societies as they move through the universal life cycle of birth, childhood, adolescence, adulthood, and death. These changes have long been of interest to anthropologists and other scholars who have noted that the critical turning points in the life cycle are often accompanied by ceremonial activities, such as weddings, funerals, and initiation ceremonies, which give ritual expression to the transition of the individual from one social position to another.

A half century ago, the French scholar van Gennep first called attention to the universality of these ceremonies in his classical

---

Eddy, *Walk the White Line: A Profile of Urban Education*, (Garden City, N. Y.: Doubleday Anchor Books, 1967 and New York: Frederick A. Praeger, 1967).

[7]Howard S. Becker, "The Career of the Chicago Public School-Teacher," *The American Journal of Sociology*, 57 (1952), 470–477.

cross-cultural study.[8] Calling them *rites de passage,* van Gennep noted that most of these rituals have three components—separation, transition, and incorporation—and provide a symbolic expression of the actual changes in the relationships of the individuals to others in their society. Examples drawn from the familiar ceremony of a wedding in our own society will serve to make more explicit the connection between critical alterations in one's social relationships and the rites symbolizing them.

In all societies, the marriage of one individual to another is usually accompanied by a marked reduction or even cessation of interaction between the individual and the groups with which he was formerly identified. In American society, for example, it is common for the young man or woman who marries to leave his or her own family and place of residence and to establish a separate home and family. In our religious and civil ceremonies the act of the father or other close relative giving the bride away may be viewed as symbolic of separation from or decreased interaction with her own family as a result of marriage. Similarly, the bachelor dinner and the bridal shower are ceremonial expressions of the alterations in relationships to peers of one's own sex which will come about as a consequence of marriage.

As the individual begins to make the transition from the status of being single to that of being married, he is in a critical state. He has severed his former relationships with others, but has not yet become a part of the new group into which he is moving. He is neither fish nor fowl. He has lost his former status but has not yet acquired a new one. During this phase the individual begins to learn about the behavior which will be expected in his new status. Symbolically, the wedding ceremony takes note of this phase by providing for the couple to pledge their troth publicly to each other and repeat the mutual responsibilities involved in marriage.

The incorporation of the individual into his new status as a married person concludes the social movement which the act of marriage implies. In this phase the person begins to interact again with the members of his community, but in his new position. Again, the marriage rites symbolize the new behavior and position of the individual in his relationships to others. The officiating clergyman

[8]Arnold van Gennep, *The Rites of Passage* (Chicago: University of Chicago Press, 1960). For a discussion of van Gennep's contribution to theory and methodology in anthropology, see Solon T. Kimball's biographical sketch of him in the *Encyclopedia of the Social Sciences.* See also Frank W. Young, *Initiation Ceremonies* (Indianapolis: The Bobbs-Merrill Co., 1965); Eliot D. Chapple and Carleton S. Coon, *Principles of Anthropology* (New York: Henry Holt & Company, 1942).

pronounces the couple man and wife and acts on behalf of both the church and the state in officially announcing the couple as married and having a new position in society and a changed relationship with others.

From the insights of van Gennep and others who have subsequently concerned themselves with rites of passage, it is clear that these ceremonies have a profound significance for individual and social identification. Of the three phases, that of transition is the time most laden with insecurity and anxiety for the individual and for those associated with him. Separated from former meaningful relationships, these are the moments, weeks, months, or even years when the individual is most in danger of losing all significant connections with others as a result of his own action or that of others. Consider, for example, the loss of individual and social identity for the bride who is left at the altar or for the bridegroom who leaves her there.

The successful movement from a period of transition requires the incorporation of the individual into the new group and status. In primitive societies, this often meant a reintroduction into a community from whence one came, but with a change of status, activities, and associates. In modern societies, it increasingly means an incorporation by those who cannot be counted as family, friends, and associates. The young couple who, shortly after marriage and honeymoon, leave to establish themselves in the husband's new work location is but one illustration of the greater social discontinuity of our society in contrast to primitive societies or even small-town America. It is important also to note that even though persons may be physically intermingled with members of the new group and may struggle for individual and social identification, this cannot be realized unless others accept them.

Historically, an analysis of rites of passage has been primarily used to provide an understanding of the individual's life crises as they affect his relationships to his family in his passage from birth to death.[9] Yet similar rites occur when individuals are inducted into religious groups, fraternal organizations, political office, occupational groups, gangs, and institutions.[10] In these latter types of situa-

[9]See W. Lloyd Warner, A Black Civilization, rev. ed. (New York: Harper and Bros., 1958) and The Living and the Dead: A Study of the Symbolic Life of Americans (New Haven: Yale University Press, 1959).

[10]See Everett C. Hughes, "Social Change and Status Protest: An Essay on the Marginal Man," Phylon, 10 (1949), 60–65; Howard S. Becker, Blanche Geer, Everett C. Hughes, and Anselm L. Strauss, Boys in White (Chicago: University of Chicago Press, 1961); Erving Goffman, Asylums (Garden City, N. Y.: Doubleday Anchor Books, 1961); Elizabeth M. Eddy, "Rites of Passage in a Total Institution," Human

tions, the terms *ritual* and *rite* are not to be understood in the restricted sense of the formal aspects of a religious service, although these would be included. Rather, the terms are used in the broader sense of "any social behavior performed for the sake of expressing a certain meaning or meanings of importance to the group concerned."[11] It is in this sense that *ritual* or *rite* will be used in this book in considering the induction of the beginning teacher into the school during the first semester of teaching.

Those familiar with the contemporary educational system may well wonder what relevance the rites of passage of primitive tribes or even modern societies have to those who enter the teaching profession. Certainly new teachers are not participants in dramatic ceremonies, which with song and dance symbolically express the end of student days and the beginning of the teaching career. On the contrary, when they refer to "being given a song and dance" at all, they are referring in a derogatory way to being required to participate in activities they find dull and uninspiring.

In contrast to the colorful ceremonies described in anthropological literature, the arrival of the new professional to take up duties in the school appears a humdrum affair, and, in fact, it is. That this event is not dramatized, however, does not detract in any way from its importance or lessen the trauma of the new teacher. By providing a universal cultural and social analogue, an understanding of rites of passage can lead to a new perception of what happens to beginning teachers and also perhaps a new insight into how badly they are inducted into their professional careers.

As noted earlier, new teachers are essentially persons in transition. Within the school, they are gradually but firmly taught the responsibilities and activities appropriate to their new role. Several groups in the school, including administrators, specialists, fellow teachers, and pupils, attempt to reach out and claim the newcomers as teachers, and the transition period is marked by a number of ceremonial activities which ritually express the several phases of this period, as well as the meaning of teaching. Beginning with the initial formal orientation to the school, the beginners undergo an intensive formal and informal training period in which the culture of the school, with its long history, is transmitted to them, so that they, in turn, may become bearers of it for succeeding generations of pupils and eventually for other new teachers.

―――――― *Organization*, 23 (1964), 67–75; Herbert A. Bloch and Arthur Niederhoffer, *The Gang* (New York: Philosophical Library, 1958); Chapple and Coon, *op. cit.*
[11]Warner, *The Living and the Dead*, p. 104.

The chapters to follow are concerned with the manner in which new teachers are inducted into the work of teaching in schools primarily attended by the children of the urban poor. At first the focus is on the role of the school administrator in the initiation of the beginners into their professional roles. Subsequently, attention is given to the part played by other teachers, pupils, and parents. Finally, the implications of the data presented for teacher training and recruitment for the school in the slum will be explored.

2

INITIATION INTO
BUREAUCRACY

Public school teachers are civil service employees in large educational systems noted for an intimate connection between their bureaucratic structure and the teaching-learning function of the school. This linkage pervades all activities and relationships in the school. Hence, an understanding of the efforts to incorporate new teachers into their recently acquired positions must begin with the recognition that they occur within a bureaucratic organization. Moreover, the formal initiation of teachers is an attempt on the part of school administrators to train the beginners in patterns of bureaucratic behavior which their superiors have defined as necessary if the school is to accomplish its educational task. The purpose of this chapter is to describe this formal initiation of new teachers into their positions and tasks in the school so that its implications for teacher performance in slum schools may be better understood.

The autonomy of individual teachers, whether they teach in the slums or elsewhere, to plan work relationships and activities within their classrooms is largely illusory. It occurs only within the official requirements prescribed by state departments of education and local school boards and the interpretation of these by administrators in the school. The line of authority which extends downwards from state commissioners of education to superintendents of school districts to school principals and eventually to teachers themselves terminates at the level of the classroom pupil. As supervisors of pupils' work, teachers are superior in rank to pupils but subordinate to the administrative echelons above them, and especially to the principal and assistant principals in the schools where they teach. Similar to other bureaucracies, the educational system is one in which the supervisory relationship is paramount and binds together those in different positions.

Teachers are allowed few certainties and little autonomy in their work; rather, they are expected to adapt themselves to the decisions of others with respect to the content of their work and the manner in which it is undertaken. Although teachers are presumably assigned to teach according to the subjects and grades for which they have received formal training, they are not allowed to monopolize particular positions and are expected to be flexible about reallocation to other positions according to the needs of the school. In other ways also, teachers are required to accommodate themselves to the demands of an educational bureaucracy over which they have little control.

Teachers are required to abide by the rules and regulations which others have formulated so that there may be a standard solution to problems and an equal treatment of persons in the school. In addition, they are required to state these rules to the pupils, and enforce them. Written records of administrative acts, decisions, and rules are provided for teachers as guidelines for their behavior in the classroom. These, together with oral directives about their work, set crucial limitations upon the independence of teachers in the classroom. Administrators likewise attempt to insure that teachers perform their duties appropriately by requiring them to keep systematic written records and to make oral and written reports about their own and their pupils' classroom performance.

Another limitation on the autonomy of teachers occurs as a consequence of the fact that teachers do not themselves own or control educational facilities and materials. Rather they are subject to the regulations of others with respect to the use of classrooms, books, and other property defined as belonging to the school. Even the type of classroom, books, and other supplies furnished to teachers is arranged by others, and teachers themselves usually have little choice in these matters.

During the early months of their teaching careers, the bureaucratic boundaries on teacher autonomy in the classroom are made quite specific to the newcomers. School administrators do not take it for granted that beginning teachers will arrive on the opening day of school fully cognizant of the duties associated with their position. On the contrary, formal provisions are made to instruct the novices in the rudiments of their task and the appropriate ways of behaving as a teacher. Most commonly, these directions are given during routinely scheduled events, such as orientation conferences prior to the opening of school, observations by school administrators and specialists, faculty meetings, special meetings of new teachers or teachers of particular grades and subjects, and individual conferences.

The part played by school administrators in the initiation of teachers into the school has important effects upon teacher performance in the classroom, teacher morale, and the eventual incorporation or rejection of the teacher by the educational system. Supervisors of teachers' activities have expectations about the skills and learning teachers should have or acquire; they rate teachers' classroom performance accordingly and recommend them for future positions or, in a few cases, are instrumental in barring them from the profession. Thus their role in the acceptance or rejection of teachers is crucial, especially for those who, as beginners, are on probation awaiting permanent state certification.

For new teachers in the urban slum, the formal administrative induction into the professional role is especially important. Typically confronted with pupils whose ethnic and social backgrounds differ from their own and who are behind in schoolwork, these teachers often have difficulty acquiring the skills needed to establish a significant educational relationship with their charges. Usually, the formal preparation for teaching has not included careful training in the special needs of the contemporary urban poor. Even if it has, the reality situation of daily teaching in these schools may present the newcomers with unanticipated frustrations and social-psychological stress.

The critical questions to be asked about the formal initiation into teaching, wherever it occurs, are these: What are the rules and regulations which teachers are required to observe and enforce upon their pupils? What technical skills are teachers expected to demonstrate? What purposes are served by these rules and skills? How important are they in the rating and acceptance of the teacher by supervisors? What is the symbolic evidence that a teacher has been fully accepted by those in higher positions? The answers to these questions have important consequences for all teachers, but especially for those working with pupils who have special educational needs and problems. The remainder of this chapter will be concerned with these questions, using the reports of beginning teachers in slum schools to illustrate the initiation teachers receive into their work by their supervisors.

THE SOCIALIZATION RULES

Like all institutions in society, the school has rules and regulations which express and preserve the customary patterns of behavior expected of those who participate in its life. These rules and
regulations are intended to enable students, teachers, and administrators to have orderly relationships with each other so that the
educational activities of the school may be efficiently pursued. The
role of the school as the formal agency whereby the child is socialized for participation in adult society gives special sanction to
school rules, which are often interpreted as the "golden rules"
necessary if the child is to be educated for responsible adult behavior. School rules are commonly believed to be necessary for their
contribution to the welfare of both the school and society. Records
of "bad" behavior in school are frequently believed to be predictors
of future "bad" behavior as an adult, and the school records of
adults who become criminals are sometimes searched for what they
reveal about childhood tendencies toward delinquency.

In large measure, the rules and regulations governing the social
behavior of those in the school have evolved throughout many generations and are so much taken for granted that educators view it
as inappropriate to question them. In those instances when they are
questioned, it will be argued in response that the rules are necessary for the welfare of the child or the educational purposes of the
school. However, these assumptions are usually untested and tend
to obscure the function of the rules and regulations in preserving
the boundaries between those in different positions in the educational bureaucracy.

Administrators are charged with the primary responsibility of
maintaining orderly relationships in the schools over which they
have jurisdiction. As custodians of the educational system and those
who have ostensible power, they tend to stress the custodial aspect
of the teacher's work. Both teacher and child may represent potential threats to the smooth running of the school. The child who
violates the rules of the school is viewed as a problem, as is the
teacher who is deficient in being able to run a well-disciplined
classroom or who questions the demands of the supervisory staff.

An important aspect of the formal induction of teachers is concerned with the standards of social behavior they are expected to
uphold in their contacts with pupils. These standards are intended
to reinforce the superior position of teachers over the children to
whom they are assigned. The dominance of teachers is not derived
solely from their adult status, for teachers are also representative of

the educational system and have status in the school. They are given a special position of authority over pupils. It is they who have been chosen and especially trained for the task of transmitting to the child the formal knowledge and skills he must have if he is to successfully make the transition to adult roles in modern society. The training of teachers is designed to prepare them for their work as adult experts who are officially designated to teach inexpert children, and the pattern of social relationships in the school is one which augments and gives expression to this definition of the teacher's role.

By age and training, teachers are the socially defined and acceptable authorities in the classroom, and they are expected to establish and maintain orderly patterns of interacting with pupils so that their superior knowledge may be imparted to the subordinate learners. In the formal classroom relationship teachers initiate learning activities for pupils, who are expected to respond by doing schoolwork correctly and in the manner prescribed. It is the teacher's responsibility to motivate pupils so that they will want to learn and to control their behavior sufficiently well that they can do so. Pupils, on the other hand, are expected to come to school prepared to accept the authority of teachers and to do the work of the school according to their directions.

The rules governing social behavior in the school give expression to the differences between the positions of teacher and pupil in the classroom. Yet, these rules do not originate with teachers, but with their superiors. In the formal initiation of teachers into their work, the teacher's role as subordinate enforcer of rules is clarified. The intent and hope is that the continuity of the orderly relationships traditionally defined as educational may be preserved and that the new generation of teachers and pupils may constitute no, or only a very minimal, threat to these relationships.

The instruction of new teachers in the social rules first occurs in the formal orientation to the school, but it continues throughout the weeks which follow. The part such instruction plays in the induction of the teacher will become clearer as specific events in the lives of new teachers are examined.

Prelude to Teaching

Typically, the formal introduction of teachers to their new positions begins with an orientation conference which lasts for several days just prior to the official start of the school year. This ceremonial event foreshadows the coming activities of classroom life. The pupils are notably absent, but present are school administrators and specialists who meet with the new recruits in several formal meetings. Commonly, those who have previously taught in the school join the new teachers for the last day of these meetings, and the beginners are formally introduced to them.

The orientation conference is a ritual observance of the transitional stage that the new teachers are in, now that they are graduates of the teacher training institution but not yet incorporated into the groups of persons comprising the school. During orientation, the new teachers undergo a period of learning about their new role and acting out the appropriate relationships with others that it entails. The formality of the orientation may vary according to the organizational complexity of the school and the number of new teachers;[1] however, most receive some instruction giving attention to the routinization of teachers and pupils for their roles in the school. The following excerpts from one junior-high-school teacher's account of her orientation indicate this emphasis:

The first formal meeting was an orientation conference where the principal addressed us and introduced the new staff members to each other and the four assistant principals. . . . The new teachers' orientation manual was distributed where a fictitious Miss Smith was featured. She was wondering about whether she would be able to cope with the school and the classes and what she should do now and what she should do next. I found it somewhat helpful in setting up routines, but reading something is easier than putting it into practice.

The teacher class programs were distributed, and I found out the classes I would be teaching. . . . We then went on a tour of the building. I was in Mr. Silver's (an assistant principal) group, and we picked up our keys in the main office and went up to our classrooms for a break. We were then instructed by the school secretary on punching in and out, where our mail boxes would be, and where our keys would be. We were told to phone in at 7:20 in the morning if we were going to be absent and to give all personal data forms about employment to the head secretary.

At 11:00, we came downstairs again and had a lecture from Mr. Silver

---

[1]All of the teachers studied reported a formal orientation program, but that of the junior-high-school teachers appears to have been more elaborate than that of the elementary-school teachers. Among this latter group, some were in schools in which they were the only new teacher or one of a very few new teachers. The reports indicate that in these elementary schools the orientation sessions are less formal and detailed than in schools where the number of new teachers is larger. One elementary-school teacher, for example, reports as follows: "I was very disappointed in my orientation program because there wasn't any. I walked into the school on Wednesday, and I was looking forward to meeting all the newly appointed teachers, and I found I was the only one appointed to that school. Since I had done student teaching in the school, the principal also assumed I knew everything, and an orientation program wasn't necessary, so they gave me work to do in the office."

on building discipline and on disciplinary procedures. We were told that we could use the dean, if necessary, or a neighboring teacher to control the class, but we would be better off if we tried to gain control of a class ourselves and did not rely on outside sources. . . .

At 1:00 we came back to school, and Mr. Lanzo (an assistant principal) and the school custodian gave us a lecture on precautions against fire. From there we went to pick up our basic supplies, which were given to us in a wastepaper basket by Mr. Silver. We returned to our classrooms to check pupil records against the roll book, make out the section sheet which goes to all classes and a conduct book which is to be kept on each person in the class to keep record of their charges and commendations throughout the day, our attendance card, and some papers to put up, and start decorating our room.

The second day of orientation, we came in again at 9:00. . . . At 9:00, we were discussing school-wide routines, with Mr. Silver doing the talking. He talked about hall passing, which staircases were up, which were down, the line of march, entrances and dismissals, the procedures to be used, the duties of teachers other than classroom such as patrolling, the reception committee, auditorium duty, and meeting classes on time. We discussed fire drills and assemblies also, the procedures to be used for entering the cafeteria and the assembly, and the staircases and everything to be used during the fire drill.

At 10:00 we went to our classrooms to continue working on the records and setting up our rooms. At 10:45 we had meetings with our subject supervisors. . . . After this meeting we went to another conference where Mr. Johnson (an assistant principal) addressed us, and he continued speaking on what to do before the first day of school, how to equip ourselves to meet with the classes. This is just that we make an outline of the routines that we expect to be followed in our official classes so that we can address them and tell them this when they come in, and it would give us something in front of us to do.

After lunch, we came back and discussed school-wide routines such as lunch procedures, health and safety procedures. Mr. Lanzo did the talking now, and we were told where to get our supplies and books, the attendance and lateness routines to tell our children. . . . Then from 2:15, we were in our classrooms until 3:00.

On Friday the full faculty was back, and the principal again addressed us in the auditorium. He welcomed back the old faculty, and he welcomed the new faculty. . . . At that point, the superintendent of schools spoke on television . . . and he welcomed all the teachers back to school. . . . We were also given our buddy teachers, the old staff members who would be closest to our rooms. My buddy teacher is Mr. Panetta, and he is right next door. He is a social studies teacher who is now chairman of the math department. He's teaching out of license and has been teaching exactly one year. I spoke to him for a while, he gave me a list of places that I could write to get audio-visual aids to put up in my room, and he seems like a very nice person. . . . At 11:00 we went back to our classrooms and at 1:00

Mrs. White continued with the routines that I am supposed to teach on the first day of school. At 3:00 we went home.

Several points are noteworthy in the ceremonial of the orientation sessions. There is the clarification of the administrative hierarchy so that the recruits learn the names and functions of those who have supervisory control over their activities. Even more importantly, these administrators act out the supervisory relationship by instructing teachers in the behavior appropriate to the teaching position. This instruction includes specific directions on how teachers are to act toward those with greater authority as well as toward pupils.

The rules and regulations to be followed by everyone in the school and the procedures to be used when these are broken are described in detail. Of particular importance are those regulations relevant to the custodial care of pupils, especially those pertaining to health, safety, attendance, and behavior. The role of teachers as those who are supposed to conform to rules and regulations themselves and to transmit these to the children is made explicit. The major theme is to train the child so that he becomes conditioned to conform automatically to the expected behavior. Indeed, this "routinization" of the child is viewed as a necessary prerequisite to the teaching-learning situation in the classroom:

> The assistant principal gave us some printed materials—more routines than anything else. The whole first week of school is a routine, Monday through Friday. Every fifteen minutes is mapped out as to what we are to do. No creative work or anything—it's strictly routining, practicing the routines, jumping to something else, going back to the routines. That's all she expects for the first week.

By orienting teachers to their new position in the above ways, school administrators attempt to ease their entrance into the school by providing them with brief but intensive training in their duties and obligations as transmitters of the school's culture. This culture is one which entails specific patterns of human interaction and activity which have repeatedly been defined as educational, in the formal sense of the word.

The definition of the teacher as one who imparts the knowledge contained in a formal curriculum to the child who receives that knowledge is predicated on a model of the child as one who behaves in ways congruent with a subordinate position in the classroom. As members of the older generation in the school, it is the duty of teachers to pass on to the new generation of pupils those patterns of behavior that will enable them to become successful workers in the school. Much of the time that pupils and teachers spend together is devoted to training in such behavior, particularly in the first days and weeks of school. The prominence given to this training as a prerequisite to formal teaching is apparent in teachers' reports about their first day with their classes:

When I entered the classroom on the first day, I felt, "This is it. You're in it, and this is what you wanted." I began first of all by routinizing the class, as we had been instructed previously. I had thought about what procedures I wanted to have followed in the classroom. . . . I went through this myself the night before, many nights before the first day, and I felt I had everything down pat. . . . I felt quite elated when the children followed my instructions.

       *   *   *   *   *

Most of the time on the first day was spent in routinizing the children, getting them used to procedures for entrance into the room, for dismissal, getting their clothing, fire drills, going to the bathroom.

       *   *   *   *   *

I greeted my official class outside my homeroom. I made sure that they were in two orderly lines before they proceeded into the room. I gave them directions in the hall on how I wanted them to enter the room, and they did so. They took any seat, paid attention, and waited for me to come into the room. . . . I said that I welcomed them to the junior-high school. . . . I wanted to be their friend, and I wanted them to be my friend. But before they could be my friend, they had to follow certain rules, both the rules of the school and the rules of my classroom. I elaborated on this latter point. I expected discipline in my classroom. I expect everyone to make a contribution. The way in which such is done is by waving one's hand and waiting for recognition from me. . . .

I explained the purpose of the section sheet which was to list both commendations and charges against the class as a whole or individuals in the class. I also mentioned my own conduct book, each individual having two pages reserved for him or herself, clean pages on which commendations or charges can be made. I stressed that I prefer the former, commendations, rather than the latter. The class then proceeded to select temporary officers. Other official class business was conducted. . . .

The remainder of my hour and a half with my official class was spent in going over the structure of the school and how the class can get to rooms as a group. Passing in the hall was discussed, the line up, boys at the beginning in two double lines, girls behind and in two double and orderly lines. The president of the class is at the head of the line and the vice-president at the back of the line. I was somewhat relieved to hear the bell ring at 10:30, for by then I had exhausted what I had to say to my official class. My official class then proceeded to their first subject area. They lined

up as I had directed them, proceeded out of the room in an orderly manner. As I stood in the hall during passing, I felt some sort of pride knowing
that I had established my authority in my official classroom.

The importance given the routinization of the child according to
prescribed formulae which the teacher is to make explicit and enforce expresses the bureaucratic values of the educational system
and ensures their continuity. The lining up of the children and the
formal patterns of interaction between teachers and pupils are
ceremonial expressions of the educational hierarchy, wherein each
lower office is under the control and supervision of a higher one. As
teachers and pupils act out their subordinate places in the educational system, they also become socialized to accept the view that
for teaching and learning to occur these formal ceremonial relationships are necessary. Other phases of the teacher's induction into his
or her work are likewise concerned with the formal behavior essential to education, and it is important now to consider those relevant
to classroom instruction.

THE TEACHER TECHNICIAN

In the modern school, formal classroom instruction is increasingly
planned by those who are remote from the actual classroom. The
common image of the teacher as the one who plans and determines
the lessons to be taught is true only in a very limited sense. More
accurately, teachers are educational technicians who implement
the presentation of a curriculum which others have defined as educationally valuable for the child if he is to acquire the skills needed
by adults in our society.

The technical aspects of the teacher's work are underscored first
by the training institutions which they attend and secondly by their
role in the educational system. The formal training of teachers prepares them as specialists who teach specific subjects to children of
a specific age. Teachers in training freely choose the age group and
subjects they wish to teach. Once the choice has been made, however, the training program primarily prepares them to work within
the selected boundaries and makes no claim to equip them to fill
other types of positions in the educational system without further
training.

In the educational system itself, teachers rarely participate in the
official definition of the curriculum or the sequence and ways in
which it is to be presented. Rather, they are expected to follow the
guidelines provided by supervisory authorities. The formal cur-

riculum is given to the teacher in the pre-packaged form of curriculum guides, textbooks, and, in some cases, lesson plans which carefully outline the activities for children graded according to age and ability. The role of the teacher is to initiate the prescribed activities in the classroom and supervise the work of pupils so that they may learn the skills and acquire the knowledge which will enable them to undertake the more difficult work of the next grade.

Thus a significant portion of the administrative initiation of teachers into their work is devoted to training in the work procedures to be followed so that the child may be educated according to the blueprints of the local school system. These blueprints represent an elaborate design for the total educational processing of all the children in the system. Teachers are perceived as those who must perform their specialized tasks effectively and without trespassing on those allocated to others if the entire program is to be coordinated. As a consequence, the initiation of the teacher emphasizes the need for classroom activities which are in accordance with the educational plans of the system as a whole. This stress is evident in many ways, but especially in the requirements for classroom displays and plan books. The instructions beginning teachers receive about these two matters will indicate critical aspects of the formal behavior required of the teacher technician in the contemporary school.

The Room Essentials

In the urban school system, and in educational theory generally, it is viewed as highly important for teachers to provide a good working atmosphere in the classroom so that the goals of education may be accomplished. The formal teacher-pupil relationships described earlier are but one aspect of this emphasis; it is also expressed by the requirements for the physical arrangements and appurtenances of the classroom.

The ideal classroom is administratively perceived as one which "reflects the teaching-learning situation." The physical arrangements should include "learning corners" for each of the curriculum areas, a bulletin board display of materials and pupils' work related to the curriculum, and room decorations of various kinds. In addition, items related to classroom routines and management are to be given a conspicuous place. Usually teachers are allowed freedom in the creation of displays and their arrangement, but the required types of displays are specified by official publications of the board of education and directives from school administrators. The elementary-school teacher has a considerably wider range of curriculum categories to cover than the junior-high-school teacher, who generally teaches only one or two subjects.

The following are examples of the types of instructions which teachers receive about displays:

Every class must have a social studies bulletin board, and it must take up the largest area of bulletin space in the classroom. Then there are certain essentials which must be around the room, such as the alphabet chart, which must be in front of the room above the blackboard. Then we must have a time line above that in the front of the room, and we must have the pledge of allegiance up near the flag. Also we must have a large attendance envelope where we put our attendance sheets near the door, and we must also post the school code of behavior.

Then there are other essentials which must be around the room. We have to have a "Before and After We Paint" sign near the easel. We should have a color chart and some sort of chart checking off health habits. That takes care of the bulletin board.

Also every room must have a library corner. As for the arrangement of furniture, it is moveable furniture, but the principal likes the children to be facing the chart board. . . .

*   *   *   *   *

Each room is to show the areas that are going on in the classroom. You have to have a special section for reading, a special section for art, a science corner, and a math corner. . . . It didn't matter what corner of the room you had them in as long as they were evident in your room and you had met the requirements.

*   *   *   *   *

The teachers are expected to exhibit evidence of the children's work in every area that they are in.

*   *   *   *   *

During the past week I received the following memorandum from the assistant principal. It reads as follows: To: Teachers of the English Department; From: Susan Thompson, Assistant Principal. . . .

. . . We should start now to reflect upon the question: How does the classroom reflect the teaching-learning situation? Will you be good enough to check your bulletin boards in order to evaluate how they show what is going on at present and what will be going on in the near future? Please check yourself upon the appearance of your classroom as it tells the teaching-learning situation in your room.

1. Pupil's work is on display in my classroom.
2. Charts for reminding pupils of their responsibilities and routines are on display in my classroom.
3. All materials on display are clear and accurate.

4. Bulletin boards reflect appealing reading and writing activities in the classroom.

5. Bulletin boards reflect outside activities that are shared in the classroom.

6. Bulletin boards include materials that reflect the class or small group activity such as an experience chart evaluating a class trip.

7. Bulletin boards reflect individual children's interests.

8. Bulletin boards are covered with commercially prepared materials only.

9. Bulletin boards have not been completed in my classroom because——

Classroom displays graphically reflect the progress of the class. Thus bulletin boards, interest centers, and other decorations are regarded as constant displays, but they are to change over time. The requirements change according to the grade level of the child, and within a given year the classroom display changes so as to reflect the new topics studied and the new skills taught and learned as the class progresses. Teachers are frequently instructed that their bulletin boards should be "up-to-date" and are criticized by their supervisors if they fail to keep them so.

The Classroom Work Plan

It has already been indicated that as supervisors of pupils' work in the classroom, teachers are expected to be competent in the techniques of planning work activities for those under their supervision. Following the educational guidelines provided by local and state authorities prescribing what is to be taught to those in a particular grade, teachers are required to plan and assign classroom work conforming to the general requirements specified by those in supervisory positions above them. These requirements pertain primarily to the subjects to be taught, the time to be allotted to each subject, and the educational tools to be used.

To insure that teachers are meeting the basic requirements of classroom planning and to provide a record of the work activities in the classroom, teachers are required to submit written plans to their immediate supervisors for approval. For this purpose, teachers are provided with plan books in which they are to write up their lesson plans in advance. Collected at regular intervals, the plan book is examined by an assistant principal or principal, who, after making any comments he wishes, signs it and returns it to the teacher.[2] As a guide to the teacher, the plan book includes discus-

[2]With the exception of one junior-high-school teacher, all of the teachers were expected to turn in plan books regularly. In the majority of instances, these were submitted to assistant principals. The plan books of five of the elementary-school teachers and three of the junior-high-school teachers were sometimes or always

sion of several of the important elements to consider in planning. The description given below presents in detail one elementary-school teacher's use of these guides:

The plan book contains boxes for the subject areas. The areas are reading, and reading provides for groups. . . . Then it has a column for manuscripts and a column for language arts, oral, written, and literature. All that is on two pages, horizontally placed next to each other. Then you turn it over, and on the other side you have the arithmetic, science, physical education, health, and art.

Now the first thing I had to do in planning this plan book was to figure out a program for myself, my time allotments and what I was going to teach each day. That was the first step I thought best to take. . . . So I looked in front of the plan book and there it gave time allotments. . . for a week. In other words, for social studies, you gave it 150 minutes. Now 150 minutes is roughly 30 minutes a day, five days a week. . . . So I knew I had to have a social studies period every day. Now the music lesson was roughly 75 minutes a week, so I figured out that if I divided that in two I'd have a music lesson roughly about 35 to 37 minutes a week, twice a week, because music is a subject you don't have to promote much. . . . The children are crazy about it, and they love to do it. The same is true with physical activities. We're supposed to have an hour a day according to the time allotment, so we have a gym period which is an hour twice a week, and then the other one we make up in the classroom. So I allowed for that. The same is true of arithmetic. I have that every day for half an hour. I have reading every day for 35 minutes. I have my language arts every day for 30 minutes. I have science three times a week for 30 minutes. I have health twice a week for 30 minutes.

. . . What I'm trying to say here is that before I even began to plan the subject matter, I worked on my time allotment and a definite program. Having done that, I had something to go by. So I looked in my plan book for Monday, and it goes across: Monday—reading, manuscript, language arts, social studies. Turn over the page: arithmetic, science, physical education, health, music, and art. . . . So I looked in my program. I saw when I was going to have it, and I began to plan. . . . When I plan I keep in mind: . . . Have I asked specific questions? Have I asked questions that the children can answer? Have I correlated the areas? Have I motivated them?

Plan books vary in their details, just as teachers differ in the ways they go about "planning the plan book," but the essential ingredi-

---

inspected by the principal. In all but one of these cases, the unusual involvement of the principal was due to the lack of an assistant principal in charge of the grade taught by the teacher. The most common pattern was for plan books to be turned in weekly. Six of the teachers, however, had to submit them only every other week, and two teachers (both in the same school) were asked for their plan books only once a month.

ents are the same, and the teacher's plan book is expected to indicate coverage of the assigned subject matter, a detailed statement of the lesson to be taught, the manner of teaching it, and the educational tools to be used:

The plan book is to follow the basic pattern of motivation, aim, pivotal questions, medial and concluding summaries, homework, and any instructional materials or aids.

The specifications for classroom plans to be utilized in teaching make explicit the role of the teacher as a technician who enacts the policies formulated by those in managerial positions in the educational bureaucracy. Primarily, the teacher's role is that of supervising the work of pupils in a way that is coordinated with the educational design for processing pupils in the school system as a whole. Historically based on the application of business procedures to the organization of the educational enterprise, this design is one which places a high priority on dividing the curriculum into time units.

The model is one in which each subject is allotted a definite amount of time and taught for certain periods during the week. The pupil workers are assigned tasks which are to be completed within a given time, and the teacher both assigns the tasks and supervises pupils' work in the attempt to keep them on schedule. Pupils are viewed as being unmotivated for schoolwork, and it is the duty of the teacher to motivate them so that they will do their work reasonably well. Pupils who regularly complete more than the average number of tasks are typically assigned to "enriched" classes where they are given extra tasks to perform. Pupils who customarily are unable to keep up with the average workload are placed in classes for "slow" children and given fewer tasks.

Although the educational blueprints for the school system modify the number of work tasks and the subjects assigned to pupils according to age and abilities, these variations occur within the framework of a standardized curriculum which is to be followed by all. Teachers transmit the formal knowledge and skills required by this curriculum within an organizational structure which places them and their pupils in subordinate positions and allows them little initiative.

The ceremonies of routinizing the child so that his social behavior will be appropriate for one who is a worker carrying out tasks assigned by others provide the prelude to the ceremonies of formal instruction. By going through the rituals of preparing plan books and arranging their classrooms to meet supervisory expectations, teachers again act out their own subordinate roles in the school. At the same time, they reaffirm the subordinate position of the pupil as one who is to respond to the instructional stimuli of others by performing the expected tasks in the required way. Thus the teacher's initiation into the bureaucratic role has important consequences for the initiation of pupils into their role; for, together with whatever pieces of formal knowledge teachers are trained to transmit, they are also trained to transmit the supervisory relationship within which all formal teaching and learning occurs in the school.

SUPERVISORY SYMBOLS OF SUCCESS

The salient features of the initiation into teaching which new teachers receive from those in supervisory positions have been described above. This initiation stresses the training of the beginners in the techniques of establishing an orderly classroom environment within the social setting of an educational bureaucracy. The formal relationships between teachers and pupils are to express the subordinate role of pupils as those who carry out work initiated and assigned by teachers. The physical facilities, appointments, and educational tools of each class are to present a visual image of the classroom work as it steadily progresses throughout the school year. Written lesson plans are to indicate that classroom activities are pursued in accordance with the goals of the educational system.

The guidelines with which teachers are provided are intended to govern their daily routine in the classroom, and also to serve as criteria whereby supervisors rate the teacher's performance. By means of formal and informal observations of new teachers, school administrators attempt to assess their strengths and weaknesses in performing their duties. Moreover, supervisors often intervene in the events of the classroom and attempt to help the teacher perform according to the educational model established by school authorities. These interventions are important in the continuing on-the-job training of teachers in the types of activities which supervisors view as symbolic of successful teaching, and in the feelings of success or failure which new teachers experience as a consequence of supervisory reaction to their efforts.

Before turning to the details of the supervisory evaluation of teachers, it is important to understand that all social institutions have formally institutionalized symbols which are intended to emphasize the unity and commitment to the institution of those who participate in its life. These symbols may or may not reflect the actual situation. What symbols express may be what has been described as "no more than a feeling, an illusion, a myth, or a vague sensation falsely interpreted." On the other hand, that for which symbols stand may be "as real and verifiable as the rock of Gibraltar."[3] The outward and visible sign of a symbol is only one of its aspects. Of chief importance is the interpretation of the sign and the positive or negative feeling which it evokes.

Within the educational system, the formal social behavior required of pupils and teachers, classroom displays of work activities, and teachers' plan books are only three of the visible signs which play an important part in establishing and maintaining supervisory relationships and in making explicit that the staff and pupils of the local school are joined with others in the school system in their educational task. These three signs are of special relevance to the induction of new teachers because they so vividly set forth important beliefs about the school and what happens in it and about the people in the school and what they do. An examination of their symbolic function in the evaluation of the teacher will increase an understanding of the ways the teacher is initiated into the educational bureaucracy.

Classroom Control

The priority given to socializing the child for work in the classroom has already been described. It is not surprising, therefore, that supervisors regularly observe teachers in order to assess their ability to control children in such a way that they behave according to the prescribed model. The following accounts by two junior-high-school teachers of their formal conferences with supervisors after an observation visit will indicate the emphasis given to the socialization of the child in evaluating the teacher.[4]

Next he brought out the room appearance and suggested the improvement of its contents, for instance signs and charts. . . . Another point was to set up a list of these socialization rules. Basically he was discussing the setup for what he considers a good teaching atmosphere. The four socialization musts were, first, to raise two fingers, elbow on desk, to gain recognition. Second, to stand, face the majority of the group when speaking.

[3] Warner, *The Living and the Dead*, pp. 3–4.

[4] While only two reports are presented here, all of the teachers report emphases similar to those given in these reports. The administrative observation of teachers varies from school to school and even among teachers in the same school. However, there is general agreement on the norms of pupil behavior, and all the teachers were evaluated in terms of their success or failure in getting control of the class.

Third, speak loudly enough to be heard by all. Fourth, address the person spoken to by name. As I was unable to print up a sign for the next day, I wrote these four socialization musts on the blackboard. However, the next morning, the teacher who shares the room put these socialization musts up on the wall with a chart.

*   *   *   *   *

When I later spoke to the district math coordinator who had observed my class, he said he understood my problem as an out-of-license teacher. But he said that when administrators are deciding to keep a teacher, especially when she is teaching out of license, they are not going to worry about whether the teacher can teach the subject correctly. They worry more about the discipline the teacher has in the class.

The continual pressure which is exerted by administrators for teacher control of pupil behavior becomes evident when the reports of one teacher over a period of several weeks are examined. The case of a second-grade teacher illustrates this prolonged stress extremely well:

Second Week: The principal visited the class two times during the week. I am sorry to say that both of these times were a little chaotic. I think this was a surprise to her because the previous week when she had come to the room the children were listening to what I was trying to get across. The one time she came, several of the children were hanging in the closet. This is a constant distraction. I have to constantly try to keep the closet door closed. They love to swing from the closet. We did get them in order.

The second time was when we were giving out milk. To me, the class was considerably orderly in comparison with the chaos that had existed. The children were sitting. There was discussion going on. The girls who were giving out the milk could have had a little better organization, but I felt that to get to the point where the children were sitting and waiting for their milk was a step. The next day we would work on how to give it out in a little more orderly manner. The only thing the principal said was, "Perhaps the teacher trainer consultant can tell you about a method of how to give out milk in a more organized manner."

Fourth Week: This week she was only into my room once when she was coming through the halls. At the time, I must say the discipline wasn't what it should have been. She just came in and spoke for a few seconds, trying to see if the children would all take their places. . . .

Fifth Week: The principal came into the room with the district superintendent who was especially in the school to visit the new teachers. At the time, my children were lining up for recess, and one child was causing a disturbance. . . . But the district superintendent was very nice. He came in with me and made the recommendation that perhaps lining up would be easier if boys lined up with boys and girls with girls. . . .

Sixth Week: Another important thing that happened . . . was a visit by the principal to my room for a formal observation. . . . During the lesson, one of the children happened to fall off his chair, which was wonderful. . . . The principal did come up and make just one comment about maybe if we all have our feet flat on the floor. . . .

She asked me into her office at three o'clock. . . . Her main criticism was that several of the children were fooling, which was true. Two children were writing. . . . She felt that the children were almost aggressively interested in the lesson—the fact that we have to work on not waving hands. I agree this has to be done, but the fact that the children are starting to get interested in what we're doing, the fact they're listening, almost flying out of their seats to answer questions is really, I feel, quite an improvement. She agreed with this, and said, "Well, just try to channel it so that it's a little more organized and disciplined when the children do want to give answers.". . .

Seventh Week: The principal's letter to me about her observation was very brief, and I will read it into the tape:

Dear Miss_____:

I noticed a definite improvement in your class control. I demonstrated for you how you could make it even better. Insist on feet on the floor, desks cleared of everything, and raising hands for response as a consistent classroom pattern. Watch out for repeating the children's answers. Also when questioning, it is usually better to pose the question to the class before you call on an individual.

Sincerely,

Mary D. O'Connell

Eighth Week: The principal came into my room during the Halloween party for about two minutes. Two of my children had been sent out of the room to get a pumpkin which I had been keeping in another teacher's room. The principal remarked that two children should never be sent out of the room at the same time. Evidently she had been passing in the hall when the two children were there. I explained that the pumpkin was very heavy and required two children to carry it. Of course, at that moment, the two children came back, and the boy was carrying it on his head and the girl was doing nothing. So the principal just reinforced her statement that only when necessary should two children be out of the room. . . .

Ninth Week: The children were ready to go to recess, and I was going down to the basement. The children were rather excited with all the moving in and out that had gone on this morning, and the line wasn't at its best. The principal came along the hall and suggested that my class go back into the room until they learned how to line up. It was at this point that the specialist from the Board of Education arrived in my class. The children were very restless, which was only natural since they had been told to return to their room and not take recess. There was actually nothing I could do, and most of them had to go to the bathroom. . . .

The foregoing reports graphically reveal that the single most important sign of success as a teacher is a classroom of pupils who follow elaborate ritualistic patterns of behavior which express their subordinate position. These include formalized types of posture and movement, verbal response, and written work. Administrative observers use the presence or absence of the ritualized forms of pupil behavior as symbols of adequate or inadequate teaching performance. It is commonly believed that formal teaching cannot occur unless pupils accord to the teacher the deference which the formal social norms of the school dictate. This belief may result in an overriding stress on an evaluation of teachers' performance according to the visible evidence of ability to control pupils' behavior. In the examples cited, this emphasis is articulated with such force that skill in handling subject matter and evoking enthusiastic reactions from pupils and response to the physical needs of children are given no importance.

The Classroom Beautiful

The overt behavior of pupils is but one of the signs employed by administrators to assess teaching performance. A second, even more readily visible and standardized sign is the appearance of the classroom. Classrooms are periodically inspected by administrators in order to determine whether or not teachers have set up the types of displays deemed to be necessary if the classroom is to fulfill its educational goal. Teachers found to be deficient in this respect are reprimanded.

The meticulous attention given to this aspect of the teacher's performance is apparent in many situations, of which the following are a few examples:

Recently the painters had been in, and they had pulled down many of the things around the room. I hadn't had the chance to put some of them up, especially the time line which the principal stresses so much. . . . So he was very disturbed that I didn't have the time line up.

*   *   *   *   *

Everything was fine about my lesson, but the principal said that the decorations were nice in my room but that I should have more, and in brighter colors. For example, I have green paper on the bulletin board, and he said I should get bright colors. So what I did Friday was rip it all off. . . . I am going to paint it yellow so that it will be bright and put a border on it and then hang up the things that I have . . . so that it will look nice and neat and be much better.

*   *   *   *   *

The principal is a bug on plants on the window sills, but I never realized how much of a bug until he observed me teach. He said, "You have a plant on your desk, and you are such a lovely young person you should have plants on the window sills. . . ." So I don't know, I'll have to find a way to get some plants on my window sill. . . . He liked the bulletin board on measuring . . . but he said I should have had the children's work instead of posters on the health and safety bulletin board.

The necessary change of bulletin boards over time and regular inspection of them are especially evident in the report of a junior-high-school teacher who had been in many classrooms in her school:

The classrooms that I have seen are very well decorated. The teachers were supposed to have all their rooms decorated and bulletin boards fixed up by the third week of the term. The assistant principals and other supervisors walk around and check and look at the bulletin boards and see the various work that is up.

Now there is more of the classwork up and more tests up. Before, for instance, if the bulletin board was on science, there were various pictures of experiments and science in the news, current events, the junior-high-school code of behavior and things like that. Now it's becoming more of a display of the outstanding work of the class, whether it's in social studies, art, math, or science. You see the children who have got very good grades, and their papers are exhibited on the bulletin board on the side of the room. So before it was mostly pictures, and now you see much more classwork up. Many of the teachers have added much more to their rooms because supervisors have come around and stated that certain things were missing in their exhibits and that they should have more things up to interest the children. I notice that each room, regardless of the subject, has a current events bulletin board up. One thing that I have noticed in these classrooms is that, especially in social studies, most of the bulletin boards look the same. . . .

The decoration and arrangement of the classroom so as to present a favorable image is not exclusively a matter of supervisor-teacher relationships within the school. It also involves public relations. Thus, when parents are invited to visit the school for "open school week" or when school officials from outside the local school make visits, teachers are particularly urged to "fix their room up" so that the success signs are prominently displayed:

At the last meeting, they said, "Parents are coming next week. If your room is barren, please fix it."

* * * * *

In preparation for the parents' visit, my classroom was especially deco-

rated. . . . Every bulletin board was covered. The bulletin boards on the
closets had examples of the children's best work. . . and these were marked
with special types of recognition—stars, stickers, different types of checks.
In the back, along the cabinet ledge which runs across the entire back of
the room, there were individual folders made by the children and decorated by the children with any type of picture they would like. Their
names were on the bottom, and these held all the work that the children
had done during the term so far. It had some of their homework. . . . It had
handwriting specimens, types of arithmetic, and samples of art work that
the children had done. These were arranged in order, starting at the beginning of the term, showing the improvement. . . .

                *   *   *   *   *

There were two men from the Board of Education coming. . . . Just in
case they might come to my room, I put up all new current events because
I have current events two weeks old, and I changed "Our Best Work." I
put up some new papers. I took down the Thanksgiving bulletin board and
put up a health bulletin board. This was all done in ten minutes in the
morning. . . . I said to the kids, "Alberto, take down the bulletin board.
Carlos, put up these articles. The people from the Board of Education
might come to see us."

                *   *   *   *   *

We were issued directions in our mailbox last week that our rooms will
be inspected for Open School Week and that we should finish whatever we
were doing to decorate our rooms as early as possible.

The display of classroom activities is oriented toward the presentation of the ideal classroom in which children make progress and
perform their tasks well. The criteria for the acceptance of children's work for display typically indicate that the work must be of
especially good quality or demonstrate improvement. Written compositions, for example, must be neatly written or have been copied
after the teacher has corrected them if they are to be displayed.
Similarly, only the better examples of other types of work are apt
to be chosen.

The classroom display is intended to present a favorable image of
the classroom to administrators and outsiders and reward the child
who does well. It is also a symbolic portrayal of the essentials of the
ideal classroom, which include a number of factors. First, there is
the element of children working in all areas of the curriculum appropriate for their grade and continually learning new skills and
understandings. As bulletin boards and other parts of the classroom
display change over time, they reflect the progress of children as
they move on to more advanced phases of the curriculum. Secondly, the ideal is a classroom wherein the orderly behavior sum-

marized in charts of school rules is followed and to which children come properly groomed and having had the breakfast prescribed in the health displays. Thirdly, the model is not a classroom existing in isolation from the world but one which keeps up with world events, participates in the celebration of national holidays, and daily pledges its allegiance to its country. Finally, the ideal is a classroom where individuals are recognized and their contributions to the work and life of the school rewarded.

By displaying the appropriate and required visual materials for supervisors and others to see, teachers express their commitment to the ideals of the educational system and the progress of the class toward these ideals. Implicitly the assumption is that the teacher has done his or her job well or such materials would not have been displayed. Supervisors interpret the outward signs provided by educational artifacts as indicative of work in the classroom which conforms to the aims of the school. Discrepancies between the institutional display of educational activities and the social facts of life in the school may be known to exist. However, the use of the signs continues to be important as a means of making explicit the educational goals as well as the supervisory relationships within which they are to be achieved. The teacher who wishes to be considered successful must learn to display the signs effectively, even if they do not accurately reflect what is transpiring in the classroom.

The Formal Lesson

The third important sign used to evaluate the work of the teacher is the plan book, which must be regularly submitted to school administrators for approval. The inspection of plan books is intended to provide teachers with professional help, but it is often solely or primarily concerned with whether or not the teacher is following the required form in presenting formal lessons to the class. The following reports of beginning teachers on the comments made by supervisors about their plan books indicate the chief criteria used in appraising plan books:

I should have included a name for each reading lesson.

* * * * *

I was putting down the book and the page, but the assistant principal said I should write down the contents so that she doesn't have to look at all those books to see what I am teaching.

* * * * *

The only comment the principal had on the plan book was "very good."
Then he had the words *music* and *art* underneath it. I guess this is because
this week I did not have music and art in my plan.

        *   *   *   *   *

The first week, the only comment was that I hadn't given a recess plan,
and once I mentioned a story and didn't give the author. I use the regular
teacher's plan book with the time blocks, and I have always put in the aim.
. . .I know the principal looks for the aim.

        *   *   *   *   *

The last plan book he marked, "good class planning." Another time he
wrote, "What is your reading follow-up?"

        *   *   *   *   *

I got a note from the assistant principal telling me that I have to set up
my math in a different form. I have to have the aim, reinforcements, en-
richment, and something with an *s*. I can't remember.

        *   *   *   *   *

I had a few problems with my plan book last week. I have a science
coordinator who comes in for two hours a week. I'm supposed to cover
science in my plan book, and I didn't. I have been doing it. . . from week
to week. This week I said, "I'm not going to do it. Two hours a week is
enough for them. They don't have to have more science. I am not making
Einsteins out of them. I have to teach them English first." And I didn't put
science in my plan book. I just put the coordinator's name. The assistant
principal didn't care too much for that idea.

        *   *   *   *   *

The only criticism of my lesson plan was that I didn't have enough
written homework in English, but I'll remedy this.

Only occasionally do supervisors reading plan books respond
with specific suggestions or offers to help the new teacher in carrying out the outlined plans.[5]

        *   *   *   *   *

The assistant principal read the plan books quite thoroughly, surprisingly
enough, and there were quite a few comments. She was very nice, and she
sent up a few things, posters, etc. which she thought would come in handy
with the things that I had planned for the children for the week.

[5]When the beginning teachers were specifically questioned about plan books at the
  end of seven weeks of teaching, their reports indicated that the great majority of
  supervisory comments were directed toward helping them meet the formal requirements for a satisfactory plan book rather than toward successfully putting the
  plans into action.

Beginning teachers have comparatively little difficulty in quickly learning to write plan books that are satisfactory to their supervisors.[6] The fact that supervisors cannot and do not observe the teachers' classroom activities except at infrequent intervals often means that discrepancies between lessons presented in the plan book and those actually taught in the classroom may be widespread, with or without the supervisor's knowledge. Nevertheless, the plan book stands as a sign that the curriculum is being taught, that the children are advancing, and that the teacher is successful.

ADMINISTRATIVE ACCEPTANCE AND REJECTION

The extent to which beginning teachers are accepted as competent technicians by the supervisory staff varies. Informal and formal observation of teacher performance is intended to provide supervisors with some basis for judging the teacher's ability to teach. Yet, as indicated earlier, much of this observation focuses on the ability of the teacher to control the social behavior of pupils, to perform the art of institutional display, and to write a plan book according to the required form. These three aspects of teaching performance are all readily appraised. More, however, is expected, and teachers are also evaluated for their technical skill in formal teaching. From the viewpoint of the new probationary teacher, the evaluation at the time of the officially required formal observation is of particular importance.[7] This official observation by principals and assistant principals usually occurs at regular intervals, with advance notice often being given to the teacher. Following the formal observation, a written evaluation of the teacher is made by the supervisory observer and becomes part of the teacher's official record in the school system. Beginning teachers carefully distinguish these occasions of formal observation from informal observations, which may occur at any time and are not generally announced ahead of time or followed up by written statements. So important is the formal

[6]The reports of the twenty-two teachers studied indicate that while a small minority had initial difficulty in writing plan books, this was not a continuing problem. Only one of the teachers appeared to have prolonged difficulty. This was a junior-high-school teacher, teaching out of license, and by mid-December even she had met the requirements satisfactorily.

[7]During the first semester of teaching, nineteen of the twenty-two teachers reported one or more formal observations of their classroom work. Three of the junior-high-school teachers, two of whom were in the same school, did not have this experience. Of the nineteen teachers who were formally observed, thirteen reported the formal observation as the most important thing that had happened to them during the week. The number of formal observations per teacher ranged from one to three.

observation that teachers sometimes make special preparations for
it, even to the point of threatening their pupils with reprisals if they
are not on their best behavior:

In the beginning I was nervous. I'm always nervous when a supervisor
comes. But I knew what I wanted to do and how I was going to do it, and
it worked out pretty well. Also, the children were behaving beautifully,
and I had given them a special warning, and this was why they behaved
so nicely.

On Wednesday afternoon I told them that the principal was coming in
to watch them Thursday morning before report cards are given out. He
had to see which children really belong in the fifth grade and which had
to go back to the fourth grade. I said, "He's going to be watching your
work to see how smart you are and if you can answer in class. He's going
to be looking at your behavior. And this, of course, scared them. I didn't
know whether it would or not, but it really did, and I reminded them
Thursday morning about it. When he walked in, it was dead silence in the
room. I really had never seen anything like it in my life. They were scared
out of their pants, and they responded beautifully.

They really gave out materials nicely, and they did their work nicely.
And a lot of the children who usually sit and don't respond so much were
responsive. The funniest part was when he walked out of the room, they
all gave one big sigh of relief. Not that they're that terrible all the time, but
you know when the supervisor is there you want them to be especially
good, and this really worked. I don't know how legal it was. Maybe it was
sort of giving a false impression. I just felt it was important, and it worked.

Whether formal or informal, these contacts with supervisory personnel are occasions on which teachers feel either supported or not
in their new professional roles. Hence they are extremely important
in the administrative initiation of teachers into their work. The
excerpts cited below are from the reports of one teacher who, after
a few weeks in the school, was chosen by her supervisors as a model
teacher. They provide an introduction to a fuller understanding of
what a successful transition into the ranks of those who are administratively acceptable entails.

Second Week: On Tuesday morning the principal made the grand tour
of his new teachers without any forewarning. My class was busily engaged
in studying the words of the week. . . . All of a sudden, the door opened
and in walked the assistant principal, who is my grade supervisor, and with
her was the principal, who made a tour of the room, noting what was on
the blackboard, the bulletin boards, the general makeup and discipline of
the class, seeing if they were prepared to do their work, etc. Before he left,
he gave the class the usual rah-rah pep talk, how nice they all looked, how
well he knew they were going to do this term in the third grade and how

important the third grade is and this sort of thing. . . . He seemed quite pleased with the decorum I had established in the classroom, the work that was being done, etc. I guess this is a usual procedure to make you feel good about it. He succeeded in proving his point.

Fourth Week: The district superintendent happened to be in our building, and the principal brought him into my classroom, and he looked around and asked the children a few questions. . . . The district superintendent seemed quite pleased with what was going on and checked the bulletin board displays, etc., of my classroom, and then they left.

Fifth Week: Another reason I think the children enjoy making the picture dictionary is that the principal came in one day when we were writing one of these stories, and he seemed to show the class how impressed he was with the work they were doing. He asked us if, when we had finished with it, he could possibly have it to show all the other teachers and classes.

Thirteenth Week: The most important thing that happened to me this week, I guess, would be considered my observation by the principal and the assistant principal. . . . Afterwards, I had my relief period so he invited me to come down for coffee in the office and I went down. He seemed quite delighted with the whole thing. It seems that I have been trying most diligently to get the children to learn the different means of word attack, such as root words and endings with the compound words, finding two little words in a big word, word families such as *hat, cat, bat*, etc. Whenever I introduce the new words in the basal reader, I use as many of these word-attack skills as the words necessitate. . . . He was quite pleased with this. I usually give them riddles after we go through the words, and they come up and put the circle or line under the word so that they are actively participating in it and this he liked. . . .

The class was really most actively involved, and he liked the fact that while they were doing this, I was walking around, and I was helping the children with the words or would stop and listen to a few children while they read. . . . And practically everything really proceeded just as smoothly as normally. I know the children at the beginning of the term were pointing at the individual words so I now have them using book marks, so as they move down the page they move the book mark down. So this has alleviated the pointing to a great extent, and they are now able to grasp phrases or at times even a complete sentence if it is a short sentence. And he liked this idea.

One of the things I'm trying to stress now is speaking distinctly and loudly and stand when you read. It just so happened that one of the boys sort of mumbled an answer, and I asked one of the other children if she had heard it, and she said, "No." Five minutes later when it was her turn to speak she was also sort of speaking in a low voice, so I made a joke out of it, and I said, "Helen, you said you couldn't understand Robert so why don't you speak a little louder?" And it was little things like this that he enjoyed most, because I was more or less anticipating problems and trying to get them solved, and I was doing it more or less in a jovial frame of mind, not a scolding sort. . . . It was things like this that were pointed out to me, which the principal and assistant principal said were exactly what they were looking for. . . .

The one criticism he had was that I hadn't repeated the motivating question right before they started to read the story. I reminded him that on the board was the first question that the children knew they had to look for, so his whole critique was more or less out the drain. So he asked if it was all right with me if he found some little meagre points to pick on because he had to do something.

Fourteenth Week: The principal and the assistant principal made a grand tour once again, and it just so happened that at the time I was doing a lesson with money value with the children, and they seemed rather happy to see what was going on. Most of the children were eagerly participating. The hands were up, and they were all taking an active part in the lesson, contributing and asking questions, etc., solving problems that I had posed for them.

My next-door neighbor, one of the teachers who is also on probation now although she has been teaching in the school for three years, has been having a pretty rough time of it this year. She has a hard class, and they've been pretty rotten, and the principal is certainly not giving her too much of a firm backing. He brought her into the room to see how my room was set up and to see that my children, who are not that much brighter than hers, can become involved and can actively be engaged as part of the lesson. He is always bringing people in to see my room.

Seventeenth Week: On Tuesday we were supposed to have an observation by the assistant principal and the principal, but for a change it just didn't come through. As I understand it, if they are more or less pleased with the type of work that you have been doing, and the principal knows that more or less all the curriculum areas are being covered and that the children are working fairly well, he more or less won't bother you, and he won't make his observations as frequent as they do in a good many schools. Because of this, I really haven't been bothered. I have had just one observation, and I still haven't received the write-up on that one.

The above account is a particularly striking example of one teacher's quick transition from the status of a beginner needing supervision to a model selected by the supervisory staff for other teachers to follow. The symbolic acts of incorporation include the principal's verbal praise of both the class and the teacher, his selection of the teacher and the class for observation by the district superintendent, his use of work done by the class as a model for other teachers and pupils, his formal commendation of the teacher in a supervisory conference, and his use of the teacher as a model who is to be observed by others who are having difficulty establishing control over the behavior of their pupils. Finally, there is the decrease in the supervisory observation of the teacher's classroom activities.

Most teachers are not as quickly and fully claimed by administrators as this teacher was during her first semester of teaching.[8] Others experience more moderate forms of supervisory acceptance. Still others primarily experience an administrative rejection, which is also expressed by symbolic acts. The following case is in sharp contrast to that of the model teacher:

Seventh Week: One thing that happened this week was a trip we had taken on Friday to the museum. The trip worked out much better than I thought it possibly could. First of all, it was educational so the children could enjoy it, and most of all they were well behaved. . . . We toured the archaeology exhibit in the museum, the mummies in ancient Egypt and the armor of the fourteenth and sixteenth centuries, and the children were thrilled by it. Their behavior just proved one thing: if you keep them occupied, they live up to your expectations.

I myself was thrilled because I was alone. There were no parents with me. I was taking care of the children by myself, and this worked out quite well. As far as that is concerned, I certainly will take them on another trip. What impressed me most was the children. When it was time to leave the museum, all of them wanted to stay, and they wanted to see the paintings which I had told them we might have time to see. But, as it turned out, we just didn't have time, but many of them in their compositions expressed the fact that they would like to go again with either the class or their parents. I really felt that was a great step forward as far as the children were concerned . . .

. . . The least successful lesson during the last week, as was pointed out to me by my principal, turned out to be my trip to the museum. I had not had enough time to really motivate the children and tell them why we were going to the museum and what they were to see and really give them the background. I figured we had so many things to cover, and we would get to this after the trip was over. But as it turned out, the principal came up about ten minutes after I got back to the classroom and questioned the children on what they had seen, and where the museum was located and other things like that. The children knew where the museum was located naturally, but he had asked what they had seen. One girl got up and said that she had seen armor and this was what he hit upon. He's a history bug, and he asked, "When did people wear this?" The child said, "Oh, when King Arthur. . . . They worked for King Arthur." He asked, "What age in history is this associated with?" I knew this was way above their heads, and they just had no perception of what he was talking about. So it turned out he did a time line with them, starting with the early Egyptians and the Romans and the Greeks, through the Middle Ages, which was what he was asking for—from 1200 to 1600, 1700 and through the modern ages.

Now this I would have gotten to if he had given me a free hand, but as it turned out he told me that I should definitely have a time line in the

[8]Of the twenty-two teachers, this was the only one to be claimed by the supervisory staff to this extent.

class. Yet I feel that these children have no conception of time, and what is the purpose of having it up in the room if the children don't understand? I sort of told him that we'd do it as soon as possible, but my heart is not really in it, and I feel that he's being very unfair. . . . Then he told me also in front of the class, which upset me no end, that I should have this time line and a corner of my room devoted to our trip. He wanted to know if I had assigned homework, and I said that the children were doing a composition and art work on what they had seen. He walked out without any further comment, but left me quite upset.

Eighth Week: The principal came to me just as I was beginning pre-test with the children. He observed my room and part of my lesson. He interrupted the lesson and said that this was not the way to do a spelling lesson. He told me how it should be done. I should have each child taking the pre-test in a separate spelling notebook. I permit them to take it on a separate piece of paper so that they have perfect spelling in their good spelling notebook. He said this is wrong. It should be that they take their pre-test in the spelling book, mark it pre-test and then correct it in the other column. Divide the paper into two parts and correct it. Let them study their corrections. After he finished saying what I had to do with the spelling book, he said, "Do you have the spelling manual?" I said, "No," and he replied, "Well no wonder you don't know how to do it. I'll see if I can get you a spelling manual as soon as possible."

Sixteenth Week: We have to test fifth and sixth grades for physical fitness, and it involves push-ups, sit-ups, and squat thrusts. I had never seen squat thrusts, and one of the teachers showed me how to do it, so I had children demonstrate it. Some of the children knew how to do it. There are two ways of doing it. The teacher taught me one way, and then the principal walked up one day as I was testing squat thrusts. He said, "What are you doing?" I said, "I'm testing them for squat thrusts." He said, "That's not the way to do it," and he showed me another way to do it. . . .

. . . Since my class is giving the play in a few weeks, I felt it would be nice if we had a rehearsal after assembly yesterday. So I asked one of the teachers who is a pianist if she would mind staying in the auditorium with her class to help my class with a song that we were learning for the play. And she said she would stay and that she'd like her class to learn the song too. She was in the middle of playing the melody for us when the principal walked in and wanted to know what we were doing in the auditorium. I told him that we were rehearsing, and that Miss Barrett was helping us with the tune. So he said, "All right," and told Miss Barrett that a parent had come to see her. She excused herself and left.

The principal came back in and asked, "Exactly what are you doing?" I said, "We are doing a song. We have a song prepared for the play, and Miss Barrett was giving us the melody for it." Then he said to the class, "How many of you have the words to the song?" A few children raised their hands, and he said to me, "Well, I don't think the children are getting anything from this. It's just a waste of time." So I said to him, "All right. Because the children don't have the words to the song. The children had the words, but I didn't know if we had permission to stay here after assembly to work on the song, and furthermore, the teacher who conducts the assembly taught a Columbus Day song to the entire assembly without giving the words beforehand . . . and I thought that worked out very nicely, and you certainly didn't say there was anything wrong about it . . ."

So he said, "Well I don't think they are getting anything out of it," and he started to walk away. I walked after him, and I said, "If you think they are not getting anything, I'll leave." With that, I turned around and said, "Class, stand!" He came back and said, "Oh, but if you think that they are getting something, then by all means stay," and he told my class to sit. I was very annoyed at this point. . . . To come in and tell me that he doesn't think that the children are getting any benefit out of it—that is what annoyed me, and I just let him have it.

In contrast to the model case cited earlier, this account is an extreme example of keeping the newcomer in a lowly, subordinate position and viewing her as one who needs continual supervision. The symbolic acts of rejection include the public reprimand of the teacher in front of the pupils, the censure of activities which do not conform to the principal's interpretation of the way things should be done, and the discouragement of autonomy on the part of the teacher. For this teacher, the administrative interventions result in feelings of depression, frustration, and anger and a lack of confidence in her professional competence. In this instance, the administrative initiation into teaching is grim indeed.

The important aspects of new teachers' initiation into their work by those who occupy supervisory positions have now been considered. It has been noted that the autonomy of the individual teacher in the classroom is largely illusory and that the teacher may be more accurately described as an educational technician who implements the educational program which others have decided is necessary for the child. As educational technicians, teachers have subordinate roles in the school, and their work is subject to observation, evaluation, and supervision by their superiors. The supervisory model within which teachers work does not end with them but is extended to the classroom itself, where they are expected to be supervisors of pupils' work and activities.

The ritualized forms of classroom social behavior, the classroom display, and the teacher's plan book are congruent with the supervisory model of human relationships which has become central in the contemporary educational bureaucracy. They are symbolic expressions of the intention to educate the child by a series of steps which enable him to learn from especially trained adults those skills he needs for adult participation in our society. As technical transmitters of these skills to the child, teachers are theoretically evaluated for their ability to teach the child. In actual practice, however, it often happens that teachers are evaluated according to how well they can display the minutiae of orderliness in the classroom. Thus the teacher's classroom displays, plan books, and teaching techniques are observed for the orderly way in which they are presented, and the pupils are observed for what they indicate about the teacher's ability to line them up, march them off, or keep them sitting in an orderly fashion.

While undoubtedly apparent in other teaching situations, the divorce between these signs traditionally used to evaluate teaching and learning and the realities of the classroom is especially evident in the slum school and makes the induction of the teacher into professional roles in these schools particularly difficult. Details of the disparity between the goals of the educational system and the reality of the classroom as encountered by beginning teachers are the subject of the next several chapters. Attention will be given first to the educational tools and resources available to the new teacher, secondly to the beginners' experiences with the pupils to whom they are assigned, and finally to the help and guidance received from older teachers in the school.

3

THE CLASSROOM TOOLS AND RESOURCES

In our examination of the formal administrative initiation of new teachers into the educational bureaucracy, it has been seen that the bureaucratic definition of the teacher's role is that of a technician who carries out educational policies formulated by supervising professional experts. Teachers are the educational agents closest to the child but furthest removed from participation in making the decisions that govern classroom relationships and activities. Their position at the end of a long supervisory chain, which begins in state departments of education and extends downward to local school administrators, allows them little autonomy in establishing the rules and regulations of the school, the curriculum to be taught, and the work procedures to be followed.

Still other limitations on teachers' autonomy occur as a consequence of their dependence on administrators to provide the tools and resources used in teaching. The classroom is commonly perceived as a place of work, and both teaching and learning are viewed as work which produces results in the form of informative lessons taught to pupils, who in turn do assigned tasks and are tested and graded according to their ability to indicate that they have retained what the teacher has taught.

Like most workers, teachers and pupils are provided with specific tools, equipment, and other resources which are presumed to be necessary for the production of the work in which they are engaged. Traditionally, these include classrooms with desks for each child and the teacher, blackboards, display areas, and other furnishings thought to be appropriate for children of particular ages and the subjects taught to them. Books, paper, and other classroom supplies of this nature are also considered as important tools in the educational process. Increasingly in the contemporary school, it is believed that the above types of classroom materials must be augmented by special human resources, non-teaching specialists who provide teachers and pupils with special training, guidance, and services, so that the desired results of education may be more fully achieved.

When new teachers enter the schools to which they are assigned, they encounter specific physical work settings, teaching tools, and educational resources. They quickly learn that, as teachers, they are subject to administrative decisions and policies which restrict and regulate the availability and usage of equipment, materials, and human resources. The school building and classroom may be inadequate to accommodate the pupils or even unsafe. The physical arrangement of space within the building may be inconvenient. Textbooks and other classroom supplies may be absent altogether, in short supply, or inappropriate for the pupils. Procedures for requesting and obtaining needed materials may be cumbersome and inefficient. The help provided to the teacher in adapting teaching techniques to children with special problems or providing pupils with extra services may be lacking, insufficient, or ineffective. On the other hand, all of the equipment, supplies, and help that a teacher could wish for may be amply provided. In either case, the beginners find that they have little control over such matters, and that they are dependent on the supervisory staff for what they receive and when they receive it.

Teachers typically feel that the quality of their work and their pupils' work is greatly enhanced or diminished by the presence or absence of adequate physical work settings, educational tools, and other types of help. Hence that aspect of teachers' initiation into the realities of daily life in the school which pertains to the administrative provisions for these educational supports is highly important. The details of the supervision of the classroom which are relevant to this problem will now be considered, beginning with the work settings in which teachers find themselves and continuing with their experiences in securing adequate classroom materials and help with the teaching task.

THE WORK SETTING

Even in slum areas, the physical surroundings within which the work of the educational system occurs vary greatly. Some schools are more than a half-century old and are described by teachers in such terms as "a medieval castle" or "a dusty gray building, dreary as can be, anything but an inviting structure." The extreme limitations of the physical facilities of these schools have usually been partially alleviated by the renovation and modernization which has accompanied adaptations from one type of school to another, the necessity to meet fire regulations, the change of electrical lighting and furnishings from one style to another, and the provision of at least basic minimal upkeep.[1] This description of one elementary school built in the 1890's summarizes many of the salient features of the work environment in this type of school:

The school was built in the mid 1890's and is rather decrepit. It has had a paint job in the last three years. This year they have been washing the walls in the hallways, but the classrooms are still very dirty looking. . . . We have a book room in the attic—well, it's the top floor. We have an outdoor yard up there which isn't used. I guess it was some sort of hazard. . . . We have a boys' bathroom up there which isn't used. I guess it's in a pretty shoddy condition. . . . We have a lovely library in our school. . . . On the ground floor (which is also the first floor) you'll find a boys' bathroom, the only one in the school that is in use. Adjacent to that is the gymnasium. After the gymnasium, there is the cafeteria. . . . On the second floor you have a kindergarten class and two first-grade classes, the principal's office, and the secretary's office. . . . If you walk to the rear of the building, you come to the auditorium which I think at one time was the entire school. There were doors which slid and separated the various classrooms. It has the old-fashioned stationary seats and desks with the inkwells attached. . . .

On the third floor there are first-, second-, and third-grade classes. . . . We have a teachers' lunchroom which was an old classroom. . . . And then there is the fourth floor on which there are fourth-, fifth-, and sixth-grade

[1]Of the twenty-two beginning teachers who reported during their first semester of teaching, four elementary and two junior-high-school teachers served in schools built between 1895 and 1910. One elementary-school teacher worked in a building built in the early 1920's. All of these teachers reported very little renovation except for painting, the installation of new lighting, the replacement of stationary with movable desks, and the removal of auditoriums because of the fire hazard. One of the schools had been converted from a former elementary school into a junior-high school, and two schools now used as elementary schools had originally been high schools. Two teachers working in the same building reported it to be unsafe. In all of the buildings there were severe limitations in the provision of adequate and conveniently located bathrooms, drinking fountains, assembly halls, and lunchrooms.

classes. . . . There are four floors in use in the building. The girls' and boys' bathrooms are located on the ground floor, so whenever the children have to leave to go to the bathroom they have to go all the way down.

In contrast to the schools built at the turn of the century are the modern, post-World War II buildings, which are strikingly different from the "old, decrepit" ones.[2] These are the schools referred to by teachers as "showplaces" and as having "everything you could want." As one elementary-school teacher expressed it, "It just picks your spirit up to walk into the building because it's so new and so beautiful that it just fosters learning." Some of the outstanding differences between these buildings and the old buildings are illustrated by a comparison of the following report with the preceding one:

It is a brand new school. The building is white brick and it's three floors high. All of the classrooms face the street. . . . On the first floor there is the principal's office and the custodian's office. As you proceed down the hall in one direction, there is the lunchroom and the kindergarten classes. As you come down on the other side of the building on the first floor, you have all the first-grade classrooms, and two classrooms that are going to be used for the pre-nursery school. . . . As you enter the school from the main entrance, there is a beautiful mosaic on the wall, just beautiful. Opposite this mosaic is the assembly hall.

On the second floor, above the principal's office, we have the second-grade classrooms and on the other side, above the first-grade classrooms, you also have the second grade. You have the fifth and sixth grades on the third floor. [In this school, the third and fourth grades were in an annex rather than in the main building.] Now one of the assistant principals is on the second floor, and the other is on the third floor. . . . The children's lunchroom is on the first floor. . . . It's an enormous room. . . . all the children eat lunch in that room, including the ones from the annex. There is a teachers' lunchroom on the first floor and behind the children's lunchroom. . . . I think that the very physical features of our building are an asset to teaching. There isn't one liability in the building.

Corresponding to the wide differences in school buildings are variations in classroom conveniences. Teachers in the older buildings frequently complain that their rooms are "dingy" and dirty and characterized by chipped plaster, rickety furniture, and a lack

[2]Seven of the elementary-school teachers and four of the junior-high-school teachers who made weekly reports were assigned to buildings constructed after World War II. All of these teachers spoke highly of the facilities in their schools. Three of the junior-high-school teachers were situated in schools built in the 1930's and early 1940's. Little modernization had occurred in these schools in recent years, and two of the schools were quite overcrowded.

of any assets for teaching. Teachers in recently constructed schools are impressed with the brightness, cheerfulness, and cleanliness of their rooms.[3] The extremes are well represented by two accounts, the first from a teacher in a school built in 1900 and the second from a teacher in a school built in 1954:

I can't think of any physical features of my room that are an asset in teaching. . . . It is a very dingy-looking room, a very dirty classroom. . . . It has no bulletin boards. It has a blackboard across the back which I covered with a maroon sort of burlap, and I hung things on that and use it as a bulletin board. . . .

The general appearance of my room is unbelievable. There are two supply closets. They have glass doors on them. One of them is missing glass. I have covered these two panels with oil cloth, so on the one with the broken glass there is no backing. When somebody comes by and brushes against it, the oil cloth tears. I have one wooden door—my closet door—to hang things on. Otherwise there is no place in my classroom where I can put thumbtacks.

My front blackboard is three boards wide. . . . I have one light that doesn't go on. . . . My desk is very old and decrepit. My whole classroom is old and decrepit. . . . Everything becomes a major project when you hang something up because you just can't go over to a bulletin board and stick it up with a thumbtack. You have to use scotch tape, and then the scotch tape falls down, and you have to put mucilage on it and then you resort to straight pins. . . . It takes ten minutes to hang up a picture. . . .

There's not much room for walking around because of five tables in back of the room. . . . I covered the tables with oil cloth because the first day I was there everything I wore got torn on them. . . . I don't like this room at all.

*   *   *   *   *

It's a bright, sunny, simply designed, rectangular room. . . . The front wall is covered by blackboards. When I am facing the class, the wall on the left has the door and then it has storage closets which have bulletin boards on the outside. There are three storage closets, and then the children's clothing closets. Past these closets, there is a sink with a little stand next to it and then another closet for storage.

On the back wall there is a storage closet and a large bulletin board which extends . . . about three quarters of the way down the wall. There is a shelf, and under this shelf there are little cubby holes in which the children can keep their work envelopes. On the extreme right of the back wall there is a library in a bookcase with glass sliding doors. Under this there is another storage closet.

The right wall is completely windows. We have six large windows, and

[3]Of the six teachers located in schools built in 1910 or earlier, only one described her classroom as "one of the rooms that has been fixed up nicely." The sixteen teachers who were in schools constructed in 1920 or later had considerably more positive feelings toward their classroom work environment.

these extend down to the radiators which are on the bottom of this wall. Up near my desk there is a ledge covering the radiator ... and this is a good place for keeping books that I use quite often. . . . Everything just lends itself to teaching.

These two descriptions present the extremes of the physical work settings found in the urban school. In the old buildings teachers must make the best of their situation and use displays and other materials to "hide the rather bad condition of the classroom itself," "to make the room look as atractive as possible," or "to cover furniture which is unbelievable." Often these minor changes are made at the teacher's own expense. By contrast, teachers in the newer buildings have more pleasant surroundings in which to work and do not have to devote time and effort to disguising them or making them more palatable. In either case, the work place is something to which the teacher is assigned and expected to accept without question. Similarly, the teacher is provided with specific tools for educating the child, and is expected to make do with whatever is provided.

THE TEACHING AND LEARNING TOOLS

Confronted with classes of pupils who are deficient in the skills usually associated with those in their grade, teachers in schools in slum areas have special needs for appropriate and plentiful educational tools. In these schools, there is often a sharp disparity between what is needed and the classroom supplies available. The problem is widespread, and only a careful descriptive account of its details will enable a full understanding of the degree to which this problem permeates the life and work of teachers and pupils in these schools.

In all urban schools, the supervisory hierarchy controls the supply lines. There are formal procedures for requesting classroom materials, and specific administrators or teachers are in charge of ordering or distributing them. These persons typically have primary duties other than those associated with providing the classroom teacher with textbooks and supplies. Usually there is a close correlation between the prestige associated with their primary role in the school and the type of job they are delegated in connection with school supplies.

Only rarely does the principal, who holds the most prestigious position in the school, become involved in the work of distributing texts and other classroom materials to the teacher. This task usually falls to assistant principals. In the elementary school, they are commonly in charge of textbooks for particular grades or the entire school. At the junior-high-school level, they are responsible for the textbooks in those subject areas over which they have jurisdiction. Whereas a member of the administrative staff is in charge of textbooks, one or more members of the teaching staff are usually responsible for other supplies. Teachers make formal requests for classroom materials to these designated persons. The actual packing, unpacking, and distribution of supplies is undertaken by school aides, to whom some requests can be directly submitted, with the approval of the higher echelon in the administrative supply line. School aides are also provided in most schools to rexograph special teaching materials for the teacher. Students are frequently used in some schools to deliver supplies to the classroom.

In addition to the personnel described above, two other groups are important. Curriculum specialists and coordinators who work in the school or the school district are frequent suppliers of teaching materials related to their fields and distribute them to teachers both individually and at formal meetings. Last but not least, the school secretarial and office staff has charge of the distribution of school stationery and rexograph paper.

Despite the elaborate provision of personnel designed to facilitate the work of teachers by providing them with the classroom materials they need, the system does not always work as planned. Teachers quickly discover that they have no certain control over what supplies are received or when they get them, and many teachers experience difficulty in securing books and supplies. An appreciation of these problems may be gained by examining teachers' experiences with the delivery of classroom materials during their first few months of teaching. In the first of the two cases selected for presentation, a third-grade teacher's experiences have been brought together in a timetable arranged according to the number of weeks that had elapsed in the school term when each event was reported. In the second case, the reports of a junior-high-school teacher who taught social studies to one seventh-grade class and English to seventh- and eighth-grade classes have been compiled in the same fashion:[4]

First Week: Receives curriculum bulletin: textbooks not available yet.

[4]The difficulties evident in the two cases selected for presentation in the text were not experienced to this extent by all the teachers, but all of the teachers indicate their dependency on the administrative staff for the supplies which are provided to them and when they receive them.

Second Week: Using an arithmetic workbook left in her room from last year. These belong to the teacher who was originally supposed to take the class but became pregnant. Originally there were not enough copies for each child, but she "begged, borrowed, and stole" until she got the one or two extra copies she needed. She is still in the process of testing the children to determine their reading levels before requesting readers.

She reports that she lacks supplies and that when she came into the room at the beginning of the semester "there was not one thing" with which she could work; "no paper, no books, no blackboard erasers, etc."

Fourth Week: She has received readers, some reading workbooks, a phonics book, and a social studies book. Prior to this time she has had a limited number of classroom supplies, but they are beginning to arrive now.

Fifth Week: She does not have enough reading workbooks, "which is somewhat of a problem." She has discontinued using the arithmetic workbooks but finds no great need for them. She lacks quite a few supplies, for example, art supplies, a stapler, paper clips, rubber bands. Although she has made several requests of the custodial staff for repairs during the past several weeks, she still has two broken seats, broken windows, and a broken pencil sharpener in her room.

Tenth Week: She lacks bead boards, alphabet cards, crayons, a classroom thermometer, rulers, and other supplies. She expresses the need to gear lessons down as a result and to "make do."

Thirteenth Week: She "kept pestering people for math supplies, and they finally started coming." She has received representative materials for math and science materials that she had "been asking for for the last month or so."

Fourteenth Week: Anticipating the need for a more advanced set of readers and workbooks after Christmas, she investigates what is available in the book room and finds that they do not have enough readers or workbooks to satisfy her needs. So she "spoke to the assistant principal, and she said she would see what she could do," but as yet she hasn't heard anything.

Seventeenth Week: "The most important thing that happened to me this week was that I finally got my new readers on Friday morning when it was really too late to get into them."

*   *   *   *   *

First Week: She has her basic supplies which she was given prior to the opening of school, but she lacks textbooks.

Second Week: "I got my English books this week for my 7:6 class.[5] I had 29 people present yesterday and 30 books, leaving one copy for myself. I'm just hoping no more kids show up in that class. Otherwise I'd be missing books. I still haven't got any of my other books yet."

[5]In the junior-high schools of this study classes are given two numbers so as to distinguish them from one another. The first number refers to the grade level of the class, and the second number indicates a particular class among those on the same grade level.

Third Week: "The assistant principal in charge of social studies told me that he ordered books and they haven't come in yet, that he has something I could use temporarily . . . which is a fourth-grade social studies book. It's absolutely no help on the unit of the school or the community, and I'd say even the children in my class could read it, the entire book, within a day, slow kids that they are. Not only that, when they got the book they were so ashamed. They said, 'These are baby books.' They had them in the fourth grade, and it was an insult to them. . . .

"The assistant principal finally did give me the English books and apologized about not getting them to me sooner. So I finally was able to give out textbooks which were readers to class 8:4. In 8:9 I haven't given them out yet.

". . . . Now there are 34 people in 7:6 so I'm missing five books for that class. . . . The assistant principal has to scrounge them up somewhere."

Fourth Week: "As far as social studies goes in 7:10, I am not supplied with any current events magazines such as *Junior Scholastic*. I was told that I could order it if I could get the money from my kids, but they don't have the money. I don't even have textbooks for that class, and I keep bugging the assistant principal, and he is bugging the book company, but the books aren't in the school. . . . He said he might be able to get me half a set of one text to work with in the meantime.

Fifth Week: "I'm lacking a full set of social studies books. The assistant principal gave me a workbook to the social studies text this week, but he only gave me 25 copies of it because he just doesn't have any more. . . . A lot of their books are on order because it's a new school. This is their second year, and until they have a backlog of supplies they just don't have the money to buy everything that they need. Everything is still being ordered, so there is a shortage of supplies, and I'm having trouble getting them."

Eighth Week: "They have social studies books now. . . ."

Eleventh Week: "The assistant principal saw me again yesterday, and she said, 'Hello and p.s., no books.' I've been after her now for three weeks since they took away the reader which was pathetically under the ability of the 8:4 class."

Fourteenth Week: "I'm still without textbooks for 8:4. . . . The assistant principal told me there is a set of books for me. . . . There are only 28 copies of it, so I don't know what good it's going to do me. So I'm going to have to tell her this and not to bother to send them because it's still not enough."

The problem of obtaining textbooks and supplies is but one aspect of the difficulty teachers may have in securing appropriate educational materials. A second and equally serious problem results from the fact that, even when they are obtained, many textbooks are incongruent with the interests or abilities of the children. The discontinuity between the interests of the child and the texts is particularly apparent when older children are provided with the same readers they would have read at a much younger age had they been reading on grade level. Although the situation is not usually so extreme that elementary-school texts are used in the junior-high-school, the same reading text may be assigned to pupils of varying ages and grades within each of these types of schools. A different type of problem results from the assignment of a text according to the grade level of the child, irrespective of his ability to read it with understanding. While less of a problem with respect to arithmetic texts, which appear to be more frequently assigned according to ability, this is a severe problem with social studies and science texts, which, if given to the teacher at all, are almost always on the grade level.[6]

A third type of disparity, troublesome to some teachers, is that between the curriculum bulletins they receive and are expected to follow and the textbooks that are furnished to them. In some cases this results from the fact that the curriculum guides are written for the grade the teacher has, whereas the text may be written for a lower grade. In other cases the content of curriculum guides and texts do not coincide, even though both are for the same grade.

At the beginning of the term we were told to use our mathematics guide for grades five and six and to follow the cycles closely. This is a publication of the Board of Education. We are to work on these cycles, and the first cycle is supposedly finished by the end of November. We are to use this guide as our Bible, so to speak, and assign our lessons from the arithmetic book that we have.

My arithmetic book is a fourth-grade book. My cycles guide is a fifth-

[6]Among the thirteen elementary-school teachers, all those who taught in the third grade or above, with the exception of one third-grade teacher, received social studies textbooks. All but one of these teachers reported them to be too advanced for their classes. Two elementary-school teachers who were given science texts found them too difficult also. A third who had a science text found it appropriate, although she did not use it very much. Reports about arithmetic texts and workbooks were received from eleven teachers. Of those receiving books on grade level, four found the books too difficult, one found them too easy for some in her class, and four found them appropriate. Two teachers were given books which were designed for children one grade below those in their classes and reported these books to be satisfactory.

Similar reports are given by junior-high-school teachers, except for those with classes which are on grade level. Only two of the nine junior-high teachers found the texts for their "slow" classes appropriate. Both of these teachers were teaching out of license, as was the one teacher who found the texts too easy rather than too advanced. In these cases, there is some reason to suspect that the combination of teaching "slow" children and teaching out of license may have made them less adequate to judge the texts than the remaining six teachers who were all teaching in license and the one *per diem* substitute who was sometimes teaching in license.

grade book, and the two of them do not coincide in all cases. I object to this because the index is not good in the textbook. Anytime I go through the Board of Education cycles, I have to look through the book, page-by-page, to determine exactly what information I need to teach a particular lesson. . . . When I do my planning, I do my planning of arithmetic last. I just despise it. It takes up the most time, and I feel I'm not doing as good a job on it as I could be doing because I just don't have the correct book.

*   *   *   *   *

The children have a math text which they very rarely use. . . . It doesn't follow the Board of Education's curriculum very closely, so I don't use it on too many occasions. . . . I haven't used the science textbook all term. I received it at the beginning of the term, but it has practically nothing to do with the Board of Education's curriculum. . . . It really isn't much use to me. . . .

Even if the grade level of the curriculum bulletin coincides with classroom texts, the teacher may find that "the syllabi are for the average class on my grade, and my class is so slow that I have to adapt them to a much lower level."

Faced with shortages of teaching materials, delays in receiving them, and the frequent inappropriateness of the standard texts, teachers engage in a number of activities designed to compensate for the deficiencies. One of the most important is to become an agent for the class and hound and pester members of the formal supply line until texts and supplies are forthcoming. Although teachers, in doing so, reverse the usual supervisory relationship by initiating action, they remain dependent on the administrative staff. Success is predicated on the availability of the desired item in the school and the ability or willingness of the administrator to secure it. Pressuring the administrator is not a technique often used by beginning teachers, but those who consciously use this approach report at least some degree of achievement in obtaining the desired results:

Yes, I did get dry cell batteries and wires. I got it after about two weeks, when I finally hounded them so much that what they had to do was send it to me.

*   *   *   *   *

I finally got the map of the United States. It took a lot of work and a lot of harping with the assistant principal so he got enough push to go looking for the map.

More common than the agitation approach is that of becoming a supplier of needed items oneself or in conjunction with others who participate in the informal supply line of the school. The variety and number of supplies provided in this way is quite extensive and worthy of elaboration. Among the things most commonly supplied by teachers themselves are materials for classroom display on bulletin boards or for use in conjunction with the presentation of a lesson. Pictures and articles from magazines and newspapers and free or inexpensive charts and posters supplied by industrial corporations and other types of organizations afford a primary source of this type of material, but it is also common for teachers to purchase items of this nature or to bring them from among their own possessions. These types of things are considered to be part of the teacher's own resource file which is accumulated over time to be used for many years:

I am in the process of looking for materials, a process which began when I had the second methods course at college, whereby my instructor suggested that one start looking for pictures and all types of information rather than wait for when one actually starts teaching. I do have a somewhat extensive picture collection, and I am building up slowly but surely a collection of written materials.

In addition to money, the time spent by the beginning teacher in the preparation of these self-made materials is notable:

Almost my first three weeks of teaching was dedicated to doing nothing else than preparing special materials for use in my class. When I came home from school, my homework began—to make the things to get the classroom in order. The first thing I prepared was the number 1 through 10 on square pieces of oaktag. . . . On one piece of oaktag, I had the number 1 on the top of the left-hand corner, and then I had a picture of one cat in the middle and the word *one* on the bottom right hand corner. I did that up to ten. . . .

. . . The second thing I prepared was the flannel board. I got a big piece of cardboard and covered it over with flannel, and then I prepared the numbers 1 through 10 for my flannel board, and I stuck flannel on the back of the numbers so that they would stick to the flannel. I made the numbers out of oaktag. I colored them all red because my flannel board is a dark green, and I prepared the plus and minus sign. . . .

. . . The third thing that I made was a chart called "Class Helpers." I listed the various jobs for the children, and I made slots so that I could stick names in and out of that. . . . Then the fourth thing that I made was the flash cards, a set of word cards to accompany the words in the reader. I didn't have any, so I had to sit down and cut out oaktag and make my own word cards . . . and I have prepared a "Good Health" chart. I made this on oaktag and put the words *Good Health*, and then I listed all their names, and on that chart I put stars next to their names if they have handkerchiefs, or if their shoes are shined or things like that. . . .

Books are another classroom tool often provided by the teacher. These may be books borrowed from the public library, purchased by the teacher, or brought from home. In one school, for example, the shortage of texts was so acute that four teachers contributed ten dollars each and bought forty dollars worth of paperback books to be used as readers in their classes. In the same school, another teacher brought in many books from her home to be used as a class library. Another spent several hours searching for appropriate paperbacks to be used to encourage one of the boys in her class to take an interest in reading. In these and other ways, the personal contribution of the teacher to the problem of the book shortage in the school can be quite considerable. However, only a very few teachers exercise autonomy and initiative to this extent.

The third and final type of supply frequently contributed by the teacher is the material needed for special holiday events, such as Halloween or Christmas parties, and special classroom activities involving material rewards and prizes of some kind. Inexpensive Christmas presents, party decorations, candy, and other things of this nature are included among these contributions, which are usually paid for by the teacher herself.

As an informal supplier of a number of his or her own classroom materials, the teacher is frequently aided and assisted by two other groups in the school. Both children and other teachers may contribute or loan classroom materials to the teacher for use. Of the two groups, the children play considerably less active roles in the informal supply line than do the teachers. Their most frequent contributions are books to be used in the class library and articles for display on bulletin boards, and these are only brought in from time to time. The role of the other teachers, however, is active and commonly based on a reciprocal lending and borrowing pattern. Rexographed stencils, textbooks, and other classroom supplies are loaned by the "haves" to the "have-nots" in exchange for something the latter has that the former needs. If the shortage of goods becomes too acute, these mutual help relationships may be broken off in favor of hoarding one's own supplies and competing with others to secure what few supplies are available.

Although the material goods which flow into the classroom through the informal supply line are important, their prominence is superceded by that of the makeshift textbook. Though not exclusively used or intended for this purpose, both the "experience chart" of the elementary school and the rexographed stencil of all the schools are described and used by beginning teachers as substitutes for textbooks in the classroom. The following examples are typical of this use of the experience chart.[7]

> . . . But for science, they don't have any books to read. We have experience charts which we evolve, and they read those. . . .

                    *   *   *   *   *

> . . . I think the encouragement of the use of the experience charts shows that administrators are aware that something has to be done [about reading materials] and in the meantime, we have to almost improvise on our own. . . .

                    *   *   *   *   *

> . . . I would like a social studies book with fourth-grade topics written on a third-grade level, but in the meantime what we're doing is writing these experience charts and making our own social studies book. I'm not about ready to write my own social studies book, but this is the next best thing I can do.

Considerably more widespread than the use of the experience chart is the use of rexographed materials as substitutes for missing or inadequate texts:[8]

> . . . The phonics book is too hard for them. . . . I talked to one of the teachers who has an easier phonics book. She doesn't even have enough for her class, but I asked her if I could borrow the book and copy some things out of it and make rexographed copies for the children, and she said yes.

                    *   *   *   *   *

> . . . Some of these rexographed materials I prepared because I didn't have a textbook or workbook for the children to use, and for them always to copy an assignment off the blackboard took too long. . . .

[7]The "experience chart," as described by one elementary school teacher is a "large spiral book, approximately two feet long by a foot and a half high and ruled with an inch to an inch and a half ruling." Experience charts are constructed by both the children and the teacher and are used to introduce new words which are relevant to something the children have experienced, often in the classroom. In addition to their use as substitutes for textbooks, experience charts are also used in reading readiness programs and as supplementary aids to classroom work. Five of the elementary-school teachers specifically mention the use of experience charts because of the lack of texts on the reading level of the class.

[8]Seven of the elementary teachers and five of the junior-high-school teachers specifically refer to this use of rexographed materials. Other uses of rexographed materials mentioned are as supplements to textbooks, "time fillers" for children who finish work early, "spot lessons" that can be used for drill and review work or the presentation of accurate information, or by substitutes and unprepared teachers who must take over the class on short notice. Rexographed materials are also used as "time savers" so that children do not have to copy work down, and for evaluation of the children's work.

*   *   *   *   *

. . . of course in a school like mine, a lot of teachers rexograph material because of the lack of material provided. . . .

*   *   *   *   *

. . . I typed it up on a rexograph sheet and ran it off so that it would solve the problem of some people not having books and some people having books.

*   *   *   *   *

A lot of the teachers want grammar textbooks . . . and we don't have any in the school really, and I don't think we're going to get any either . . . so the teachers were complaining that all they can do is go and get another textbook and rexograph the material out of it. . . .

Rexographed materials are used extensively, but they too can be curtailed by a supply shortage, in this case a shortage of paper or aides to do the work of duplicating stencils: [9]

As far as rexographic materials, we're supposed to leave the stencils on the school aide's box and she'll run it off. I guess there has been quite a demand for this, however, because stencils that I've given her at the beginning of the year, I'm just getting back now . . . by the time I get them they're practically useless . . . so I myself have taken to going up on my lunch hour and rexographing as much as I possibly can.

*   *   *   *   *

As far as rexograph material goes in my school, they are very stringent with the master sheets and with rexographed material on the whole. They screen everything, and I have only used it to make copies of songs for the glee club and to make tests for my class.

*   *   *   *   *

With rexographed materials, I have to hand in anything to be rexographed a day before, and it's not that easy to have lessons prepared the day before and typed up ready to be rexographed.

*   *   *   *   *

I just type up everything and run it off, and now there is a lack of the short kind of paper that you run your questions off on every week. They tell us there is no more and that they only have long paper. I sent in these short sheets with stories on it to be run off. I got them back saying there is no more short paper, and I must cut and refit two short pieces to make one long piece. . . . And then they say, "Do you really need this many copies?" And I say, "Yes because I have three seventh-grade classes which

[9]Three elementary-school teachers and three junior-high-school teachers experienced difficulty with the rexographing procedures in their school.

comes out to 105 students, and we have no books to use, and what am I supposed to give them to read?"

The foregoing account of beginning teachers' difficulties with obtaining adequate and useful educational tools in the classroom indicates a sharp dichotomy between the ideal espoused by the educational system and the facts of institutional life. The intent of the bureaucratic system is to distribute educational goods and services equally to all. Yet teachers quickly discover, especially in slum areas, that they cannot take it for granted that they will have the texts and supplies they need for the educational task. For a few, the discrepancy becomes an opportunity to exercise ingenuity and creativity, but for most it becomes an additional fatiguing burden. For all, it represents a severe handicap in the education of the child who so badly needs the best that educational technology can offer and often does not receive even the minimum defined as necessary by those in the educational system itself.

TECHNICAL ASSISTANCE

The teacher's dependence on the supervisory staff for classroom tools and resources is not confined to the physical work setting, supplies, and texts. Teachers must also rely on others for specific help in meeting the teaching and other needs of their pupils. Although formal specific help with teaching techniques may be provided to new teachers in a variety of ways, the extent and regularity of the help given varies widely. [10] Most technical help is initiated by administrators and curriculum specialists. Teaching guides, special meetings for new teachers, in-service courses and conferences, demonstration lessons, and direct suggestions for improvement of the teacher's techniques after observation are the most common methods used to provide assistance.

[10]Among the twenty-two teachers, the elementary-school teachers generally appeared to receive more technical help than junior-high-school teachers. Only one teacher, however, received consistent weekly help. This was an elementary-school teacher working with non-English speaking children in a school participating in a special teacher training program. Both the teacher trainer and the non-English coordinator provided regular and comparatively extensive help to this teacher. Other teachers received technical aid from these and other kinds of specialists as well as school administrators, but much of this help was provided on a sporadic, unsystematic basis. For nine of the twenty-two teachers, severe and continuing problems in establishing and maintaining classroom discipline were reported as the most important occurrence of the week on four or more occasions; yet these teachers indicated that they received little or no substantial help with these problems in terms of adapting classroom work demands and procedures to the special needs of their pupils.

Perhaps the most extensive help offered is that of the pre-packaged set of lesson plans designed, at least theoretically, for use with pupils of a particular ability and age level. An example is provided by a junior-high-school teacher who was chosen to participate in a special intensive reading program designed for junior-high pupils who were between two and four years behind in reading ability:[11]

I was given an 87-page booklet to read over and to plan with. This booklet has all the plans for the days that I will be teaching my intensive reading materials to my seventh-grade class. I don't have to make out the lesson plans. The lesson plans are all uniform, and they are all made out for me. All I have to do is follow them carefully, and this was very clearly explained in the principal's office when we had the curriculum meeting.

Other teachers, though not provided with special materials, frequently find teacher's manuals and guides useful in a similar way:

I have just received the teacher's guide for the reader. It's a third-grade reader for my fifth-grade class. I've been studying that guide, and I'm following it. Yesterday I performed my first lesson from it, and it really is a fantastic thing. The children understood. They were guided, and they were motivated, and they were reading, which was the most important thing, and they comprehended what they were reading. Really the guide book is fantastic. . . . As I explained last time, I didn't know the first thing about it all, and this really explained to me how to set up this particular group, not any other group, but just this particular group. I use it as my Bible practically.

*   *   *   *   *

Now, along with the children having a copy of *Fun with Dick and Jane,* I have a teacher's edition, and this is a guide for me on how to give my lessons in the basal reader. Now I have had experience in giving reading lessons because I saw this being done in the class in which I student taught. So I really know the approach. But for the specific questions and the specific ideas and for the specifics that the children should be looking for and the way to present the vocabulary, each story has all this material in the teacher's edition, and it tells you how to do it. Now I find that it's difficult to try to memorize this the night before, so I work right from the teacher's edition. I hold it. It has the same cover as the children's, and they don't know that I'm using it, and I keep it right in front of me, and in that way I don't miss anything.

*   *   *   *   *

[11] Among the twenty-two teachers studied, this teacher received the most extended help of this kind. The pre-packaged lesson, however, whether found in a plan book given to new teachers or in a teacher's manual, is commonly used by all the teachers.

As soon as I got my math textbooks, I wrote away to the publisher and asked for the teacher's edition. I am very pleased to say that I received it on Friday, and now I can really get started. I was having a bit of difficulty with some of the problems—not so much difficulty, but I was always a little bit afraid that I'd end up with the wrong answers.

A third type of pre-packaged help is sometimes given to the teacher in the form of old plan books which are handed down from one group of teachers to the next:

When we came to school, the principal had given out old plan books which he said were very good, and I have been copying math lessons from this old plan book.

*   *   *   *   *

I have a plan book from the teacher who had the room last year. I follow her outline, which is the outline for this school, but not her plans because they don't apply to my class.

Special training programs for new teachers in the school and in-service courses, conferences, and demonstration lessons which are attended by new teachers furnish other sources of technical help:[12]

As a result of my in-service course in reading which I am taking on Wednesday afternoons at my own school, which is given by the assistant principal for the first and second grades, I became aware of an excellent aid for one's reading program. It's a pamphlet, and from this I've used effectively a number of auditory discrimination exercises, and I began a series of lessons on this on Monday.

On Monday afternoon, I call it freshman orientation, the new teachers

[12]In addition to the orientation meetings which all the new teachers attend prior to the opening of school, nine elementary-school teachers and all of the junior-high-school teachers participated in some form of special training program for new teachers during the first semester. These ranged from extended programs of several weeks' duration which included help with classroom discipline and teaching techniques to more specialized programs concerned only with the handling of "problem" children. In some cases these orientation sessions held after the opening of school consisted of only two or three meetings primarily concerned with training the teachers in filling out school forms, such as report cards and roll books, or in administering achievement tests. During the first semester of teaching, three of the elementary-school teachers took an in-service course sponsored by the Board of Education in the teaching of reading, and one took a course in the teaching of mathematics. Two took first-aid courses, and one attended a special human relations seminar sponsored by the Board of Education. None of the junior-high-school teachers took in-service courses. Seven elementary-school teachers and two junior-high-school teachers were enrolled in courses in graduate school during the first semester. All but one of these were attending the same school from which the bachelor's degree had been obtained the previous June.

had another orientation meeting at which the principal and one of the assistant principals conducted a class on the use of the reader and the best techniques for its utilization. . . . These were, of course, more or less things that we had all been doing, but it was nice to hear it in black and white and to know that you were doing what was expected.

*   *   *   *   *

The two fourth-grade teachers from my school, Miss Jones and myself, went to a math conference conducted by one of the district coordinators from the Board of Education. At this conference, we were given the new syllabus for grade four. There had been no formal syllabus, just mimeographed cycles up to now. The syllabus tells you everything that is supposed to be covered, how it is supposed to be covered, and it even gives you a sort of textbook to use in relation to what is to be covered, example problems, and exercises for the class. Of course they stress that not every class can cover the entire syllabus or even one part of the syllabus. . . . When I sat down to prepare my lessons for this week in arithmetic, I found out that everything was laid out in a most logical way, and even though there is a great deal I won't be able to cover, it will be a big help in planning my lessons. This is something the fourth grade has lacked up until now. So this really gives direction to our mathematics approach.

*   *   *   *   *

The most important thing that happened to me this week concerns itself with the *Think and Do* books. They are workbooks that the children use to try to get a grasp in the language arts area. In this book the children are asked to underline certain words or to pick out the correct word. This exercise usually is based upon the correct following of directions and being able to make association of word meanings. Now when I gave these books out, the children just wouldn't respond to it, so I went to my supervisor and told her about this. I never expected that she would come in to my classroom and give a full lesson. That is exactly what she did. She came in that very afternoon, and she showed me exactly how to work with these workbooks. This really was the most important thing that happened to me this week because it really let me see exactly how to work with the children with these books.

In the attempt to help the teacher, the emphasis on the techniques of teaching is primary. By means of teacher's guides and manuals, demonstration lessons, conferences, and courses, curriculum specialists, school administrators, and other formally appointed teachers of teachers pass on to a new generation of teachers the techniques that are officially accepted by the school system and that they themselves have found useful. However, the help provided is rarely on a regular basis and often fails to take into account the educational needs of the child. Moreover, while it may represent some adaptation of the usual curriculum for the "slow child," there is no evidence to indicate that it represents a significant departure from the traditional type of teaching-learning relationships described in the previous chapter. The very pre-packaged lesson guides provided the teacher often serve to underscore the subordinate role of the teacher as one who is to follow directions carefully so that the plans of others may be carried out.

As educational technicians, teachers exercise little control over the allocation of educational tools and resources within the school system as a whole or their own schools in particular. Rather, teachers must depend on others to provide the materials and help that they need. They often must contend with a lack of teaching resources suitable for the children to whom they are assigned and insufficient help in developing innovative teaching techniques. For the new teacher in slum areas, the consequences can be especially severe.

Without adequate educational tools and teaching resources, these teachers are frequently at a loss to know how to effectively cope with the educational task. The problem arises for two reasons. First, teachers have themselves been trained to believe that certain minimal educational props are essential if teaching is to be performed well and are dismayed if they do not have them. Secondly, in slum areas teachers are frequently assigned to pupils for whom the traditional model of the teacher-pupil relationship has little meaning. These pupils do, in fact, require not only special teaching materials but also methods of teaching different from those in common usage. As a consequence, teachers who are not encouraged and helped to develop new methods find that they frequently become alienated from their pupils. To understand this aspect of the new teacher's initiation into the slum school, it is necessary to turn now to the details of teacher-pupil relationships.

4

TEACHER-PUPIL
RELATIONSHIPS

The initiation of beginning teachers into their professional roles is not solely dependent on the administrative guidance and help they receive. Also important is the daily response that students make to teachers' endeavors to educate them. When pupils respond in ways that fulfill teachers' expectations for classroom behavior and performance, they reach out and claim the professional and personal efforts as worthwhile. On the other hand, when pupils fail to do schoolwork well or are indifferent to it altogether, they reject the professional attempts to teach them and may even bring about an abandonment of the teaching effort.

The centrality of the teacher-pupil relationship in the formal educational process is evident in the way children are said to "belong to" a particular teacher. Teachers use the possessive pronoun *my* when they refer to the pupils in their classes, and pupils speak of "my teacher" and "my class." This common use of personal terms conveys an image of the teacher-pupil relationship as a mutually friendly, reciprocal one which facilitates and enhances the work of formal education. At the same time, it obscures the fact that in reality the relationship is an administratively assigned one, usually based on organizational needs and convenience rather than on the personal choices or feelings of those involved.

The school in the slum provides particularly vivid examples of the fact that the teacher-pupil relationship is usually assigned rather than chosen. Teachers in these schools would often prefer to be teaching elsewhere if they had the choice, and pupils drop out of schools in slum areas more frequently than in other types of communities or in some instances attend only because the law compels them to do so. Pupil and parent boycotts and the demands of parents to run their own schools have dramatically brought to public attention the dissatisfaction of many in the urban slum with the formal education offered by teachers in their schools. Likewise, boycotts of slum schools by teachers protesting physical assaults by pupils have underscored the dissatisfaction of teachers with some of those attending these schools. More quietly and with less publicity, teachers refuse to accept assignments in schools in the slum and attempt to transfer to schools in other locations as soon as possible, and parents keep their children out of public schools in slum areas by enrolling them in private or parochial schools.

The special situation found within schools which serve primarily the poverty-stricken makes the pupils' initiation of the beginning teacher into his or her professional work there especially precarious. Many pupils lack the skills to perform well in school and to make the expected progress. Academic problems are frequently exacerbated by social behavior on the part of pupils not conforming to that considered necessary if the school is to accomplish its task. In extreme instances, pupils physically or verbally assault their teachers, thereby threatening their authority and overtly rejecting them. For new teachers, such unexpected responses to their work are especially devastating, and personally and professionally defeating.

The difficulty of teacher-pupil relationships may be augmented by the common practice of assigning new teachers to classes considered less desirable and prestigious by other teachers and school administrators. The assignment of pupils to a given class is fundamentally an allocation to a bureaucratic category based upon attributes which the pupils are believed to possess. Ostensibly, the most important of these is the achievement of the pupil in schoolwork, an attribute to which even age may be subordinate in the case of pupils who are allowed to skip or made to repeat a grade. Closely related to school achievement is the social behavior which facilitates good achievement or which gets the pupil classified as a "troublemaker" and one who may be placed in a class of lesser ability than he actually possesses.

Customarily, classes composed of the more academically "worthwhile" pupils are given to the more experienced teachers as a means of recognizing their seniority and providing these pupils with the "best" teachers.[1] In the slum school, this practice may have severe consequences for beginning teachers, who in addition to teaching a "slow" class may also be teaching out of license or have a class with several known "troublemakers" in it. In such situations, the beginners frequently come to regard their first year of teaching as one of non-teaching, in which their work is predominantly to discipline. In these cases, the formal educational system fails to incorporate either the teacher or the pupils into a meaningful relationship in the school.

A consideration of the activities of teachers and their assigned pupils which result in either a mutual incorporation into the educational task or a rejection of it is essential if the induction of beginning teachers is to be fully understood. To aid in this task, it is helpful to examine new teachers' descriptions of their "least" and "most difficult" pupils and the ways in which they respond to these pupils. In order that the types of pupil response which fail to incorporate the teacher into a significant professional role may be examined from a wider perspective than that often used, the types of pupil responses which do incorporate teachers will be presented first.

THE GOOD WORKERS

Almost without exception, the pupils who are described as "least difficult" by teachers in slum areas are those who do good work in the classroom or at least work hard and do the best they can. They ask intelligent questions, volunteer answers, and are generally interested in learning and responsive to the work activities initiated by the teacher. Often described as "bright," "intelligent," or "smart," these pupils have good work habits, do their homework, and even,

[1] Of the thirteen elementary-school teachers in this study, none were assigned to the top academic classes in their schools. Three taught the bottom class on their grade level; one taught the next to the bottom class, and the remaining five taught classes which ranked at or near the median for their grade. Two of the nine junior-high-school teachers taught completely out of license, and five taught completely in license. Of the two teachers who did only part of their teaching in license, one was a *per diem* substitute, and one taught only one class in the subject which she was prepared to teach. All of the junior-high-school teachers taught a range of grades and ability levels. Only three of them (including the *per diem* substitute) taught any ninth-grade classes, and only one was assigned a ninth grade as an "official" (homeroom) class. Five junior-high-school teachers had seventh-grade homeroom classes, one had an eighth grade, and two had no official class. All of the junior-high-school teachers had classes who were "behind" in scholastic achievement, and only four (including the *per diem* substitute) taught any classes in which the pupils were on grade level or above. See Appendix B for further details of the classes taught by each teacher.

in some cases, do extra work or bring in materials for classroom use.[2] They are frequently viewed as compensating for the "most difficult" pupils to be described later.

In addition to their characteristics as workers, the least difficult pupils have other assets from the teacher's point of view. These include especially patterns of social behavior in the classroom which enable the child to keep out of trouble without having to be disciplined by the teacher and to get along well with other children without disturbing them.[3] Among the many adjectives used to describe the least difficult children, "quiet," "docile," and "shy" are the most common.[4] Other frequently mentioned traits pertain to courtesy, reliability, cooperativeness, neatness, maturity, and ready conformity to the teacher's expectations for classroom behavior. On the whole, teachers find pupils with these traits personally appealing and frequently speak of them as "cute," "sweet," "lovely," "marvelous," "wonderful," "terrific," and "dolls." Two beginning teachers' summary statements about their least difficult students will illustrate the manner in which qualities of both work performance and social behavior are taken into account in classifying children as "least difficult."

The reasons I say these children are my least difficult are because they are among the brighter ones in the class. They are reliable. I can count on them to copy their work as soon as I say, "Get busy," to have it finished within a few minutes, to get out a book and read or something until the rest of the class has finished doing the assignment. They are quiet and do their work very well. They obey directions; they're responsible. I can send them on an errand, and they will give the message straight and come back shortly, without taking time to run through the halls and peep in other classrooms.

They are polite. They are courteous. The boys will hold the door. The girls will say "thank you" and "please." They ask intelligent questions during the lesson. They raise their hands. They volunteer. They are active intellectually, and yet they are not at all distractive. They seem to be always interested in what is going on, and they really have not given me

[2]A total of eighty-six "least difficult" children were described by the elementary-school teachers. In only four cases were the characteristics mentioned here omitted. The junior-high-school teachers' accounts of their "least difficult" pupils are more fragmentary than those of the elementary teachers, probably due to the fact that they have contact with many more pupils but for shorter periods of time. Of the forty-one pupils mentioned, however, all but five were at least partially described in terms of work performance.

[3]These behavior patterns are specifically mentioned for more than half of the "least difficult" children.

[4]They are used in connection with nearly half of the pupils categorized as "least difficult."

any trouble at all. I never have to speak to these children, and they're really a delight to have in the class.

* * * * *

There are so many with whom you don't have very much difficulty, and they just do their work. They come in prepared. They do their homework. They volunteer in class. They don't do anything. Not that they don't do anything. They don't do anything that is out of . . . the social norm as far as yelling out in class, misbehaving, throwing paper, or doing all those things that characterize the other students who are troublemakers.

They just don't give you a hard time, . . . and they keep quiet, and they sit in their seats, and they are responsive students. They do good work generally, and they are there to learn, and they know that you are there to teach them, and they are willing and able.

Beginning teachers have favorable attitudes to such pupils primarily because of such traits, which are significant here because they contribute to a pattern of behavior by which these children reach out and claim teachers' work in the classroom. The response of these children to teacher-initiated activities confirms the teacher's own feelings of professional effectiveness and self-worth.

On the second day of class I got a new boy into my class who is from North Carolina. He is a tall, nice-looking boy, and very intelligent I find. I happen to like him very much, and . . . I expect to have the least difficulty with him in class. He seems to understand everything that I teach the first time. He sits in the back of the room, and yet he always pays attention and does not fool around.

I have been asking the children to write compositions and he has been writing the best compositions in the class. He is also a very, very good reader. He is the best reader in the class, and he reads way above the level of any of the other children. I do think that when I feel that teaching is hopeless and that I am not getting through to any of my other children, . . . he will be a comfort to me since he does understand everything that I teach after the first explanation.

* * * * *

Another child with whom I expect no difficulty is a boy named Alfred Warfield. . . . Alfred's work habits are not particularly good. Much of his work is done hastily and sloppily, but he is extremely interested in all of the things that we are doing and many things outside of the classroom. Many times during the day, he volunteers information during a discussion. He enriches many of our discussions considerably.

One day, in some kind of discussion, we got on the topic of elephants, and Alfred told us about some of the differences between African elephants and Indian elephants—about which are more tame, which are more wild, which are better suited to being in the zoo and the circus, which were more trainable. When I asked him how he knew all these things about elephants, he told us that he had a set of encyclopedias at home which he read and that he had a lot of books at home which he read. Also, he told me that he belongs to the public library and that he likes to go there and spend some time looking for books that he takes out to read.

*   *   *   *   *

I'd like to say that the seventh-grade top talent class, which is composed of the most gorgeous little kids anyone could ever see, is my favorite class at this point, and I think they'll continue to be. As I mentioned last week, the first time . . . after dismissing them, I ran through the halls because I had a prep period, hugging people and telling them, "They're little people. They're beautiful little people." I really love these kids. They're so eager to learn, and they're just a joy to see. . . . I really like them. I find that I've been able to do more work with them. Since they are the brightest of my classes, besides doing their regular work, I have assigned a term paper to them. Their term project will be a five-page report with pictures of a famous mathematician, any era in history, and how math helped him in his career, and the importance of his work. They really seemed very eager to do this, so I'm really looking forward to their work.

Pupils who claim beginning teachers by doing good work in the class may also claim them in other ways, by helping them with routine classroom chores, discipline problems, or the tutoring of children with academic difficulties. Sometimes they show special signs of affection for the teacher or make an unusual contribution to classroom activities:[5]

Carmen Rodriguez seems to be a bright girl. She knows an answer if I call on her. She's quiet. She helps the boy next to her, who is slower than she is. She helps me when I have to write a note home in Spanish to a parent. I have one non-English-speaking girl in my class, and if I tell Carmen what to write, she'll write it in Spanish. I had occasion to send a letter home to a mother, and I had to write this in Spanish, so I told Carmen what to write and she wrote it for me.

There is also Rosa, who knows the school well and who knows many of the procedures. When I had a little difficulty with what to do with lunch money, she took the lunch card. She told me what to do with it, and she reminds me every day that she has to take it and gives me

[5]Thirty-seven of the "least difficult" children mentioned by the elementary-school teachers were described as being helpful in nonacademic ways, but this is rarely mentioned by the junior-high teachers, probably reflecting organizational differences in the two types of schools. Elementary and junior-high-school teachers seldom refer to special signs of affection on the part of the child or to unusual material gifts of the child to the class. This likely reflects the fact that personal expressions of affection and gifts are discouraged in the school.

advice. She's talkative in class, but I think she will be one of my better children. Also she seems bright, and she is well prepared.

* * * * *

Out of the girls, Martha, Joanne, and Eleanor are wonderful children. They always pay attention. They do their work. They are anxious to keep up. In short, they are not any bother at all, and I notice that they get so annoyed when the class misbehaves. They try to do their best, and they are always answering questions. They are always, to use the vernacular, "on the ball," and whenever I need help or there is a job that must be done, these children do it, and they do a good job as well.

Joanne, for instance, was my vice-president. She always made sure that the class was in order. Martha was my treasurer, and she collected money for lunch every week. She collected the workbooks, and she collected the bulb money that we are collecting for our bulbs. She kept good records and she always did a good job. Now that we have new monitors, Joanne is in charge of attendance. She takes attendance every day, and she never makes a mistake. Martha and Eleanor are in charge of my bulletin boards, and they do a terrific job. . . . I feel that if I ever need assistance in any way, I can always depend on these girls.

* * * * *

I get notes from Sally every day: "I love you, Mrs. Gimbel." "Read this note. I love Mrs. Gimbel." "Dear Mrs. Gimbel." And she draws a picture of a woman in front of the room, with examples written on the board and "I love you."

You feel, well maybe they don't really hate you as much as you think they do. And you know, after all the yelling, they don't listen to you, I guess, not because they don't like you or respect you, but they are just children and they're mischievous. . . .

* * * * *

I have one boy, John Marshall, who has been left back. He is much taller and physically better built than the other children in the class. So far he hasn't been any type of a discipline problem and has been an aid in trying to get the children to line up. . . .

John Marshall is still quite good. . . . I have placed him in the back of the room because he is tall, and he's constantly having other children come back and sit with him because he likes to help them. . . . He still is quite good in keeping the line straight. However, I try to lessen his authority along this line because he is becoming overly physical with the children, pushing rather than using the reasoning of telling the children how they should be lined up. However, most of the time John does tend to be quiet and rather shy, at least in relation to me as a teacher. If I give him one look, that perhaps he is not doing what he should be, he immediately tries to do what he thinks I want from him. . . .

In their reports about their least difficult children, teachers frequently say that the parents of these children are supportive of their professional work.[6] In a number of instances, the parents play an active role in the child's education by paying visits to the school, writing notes to the teacher about the child, attending school events, belonging to parents' associations, contributing to class parties and activities, cooperating in the supervision of homework, getting the child to school on time, providing him with such things as health care and milk and cookie money, and enrolling him in after-school programs. Parents sometimes attempt to have the child placed in a better class or retained in one class although school authorities wish to place him in another. In rare cases, they may even send a small gift to the teacher by means of the child. The following excerpts present some of the activities which make the teacher feel supported and claimed by parents:

One of the children that I have had relatively little difficulty with is a young girl, Deborah Carter. Her father just this past week came up one day. He was considerate enough. He went to the office and got a pass to come up to see me. He said that every year he comes and gets acquainted with his children's new teachers and that he wants them in school to learn and not to fool around. He realized how important school is for the children and that this may be the way that they'll rise from their station, which is exactly my viewpoint. I was quite pleased to hear him tell me that if I had any problems with his daughter I was to speak to him or to write to him.

They live around the corner from school, and he said, "Feel free to come up whenever you want to if there is a problem." Either he or his wife is always home, and they would be more than willing to discuss the problem with me. Of course, a child like this who has guidance and her parents are concerned will definitely be a child who works well, whose homework is always letter perfect, and there is really nothing more I could really want from her. . . .

I have also seen Deborah Carter's mother, but this was really a social visit, more or less. She made a big strawberry cake for the Christmas party, and she came up. She is the mother I see every day, because Deborah lives right around the corner from the school, and every day on lunch hour when I take the children over to the new building, Mrs. Carter is waiting for the children. She is really also a lovely woman, so we have more or less a very good relationship. She's been a great help to me on occasion.

[6]The role of parents is specifically mentioned in connection with thirty-eight of the "least difficult" children described by eleven of the thirteen elementary-school teachers. In only seven of these cases is the mention limited solely to a statement of the teacher's perception that the child has a "good" home background. In the remaining cases, specific parental activities are noted. Only one of the junior-high-school teachers mentioned parental activity in connection with a description of a "least difficult" child.

*   *   *   *   *

Carmen Rodriguez . . . is probably the best girl in the class, the best person in the class. . . . She's excellent in work and study habits. She goes home, and she studies, and reads books at home, and she will bring in a report. . . . She told me in the beginning of the term she wants to sit alone because she wants to be able to learn and do her work. And this is her home, because her father, when I spoke to him, emphasizes education. . . . He emphasizes being good in school, studying and working hard, and she has the same ideas.

*   *   *   *   *

Joanne is one of my best students, academically and behavior-wise. The other day I saw a man outside my door, and I went there, and it was Joanne's father. He said that he works, and that he had just come to school because Joanne's brother . . . is a behavior problem. And he . . . said, "I'd like to know how my daughter Joanne is doing." So I told him that she is a beautiful child. She does her work well, and she is all-around one of the best students in my class. Now, this man said to me that if I had any trouble I should write a note to her mother, and they would take care of it right away.

It is amazing how the children that are good have parents who are interested in them and the children who are bad, of course, have disinterested parents. This, of course, runs true to form. The children who are not neglected and who have good parents are the children who behave in the proper way and who do their work correctly.

The incorporation of the teacher by the "least difficult" children, which is sometimes accompanied by active parental support, is reciprocated by the teacher's incorporation of these pupils. One of the most concrete ways in which teachers reach out to claim these pupils is by actually arranging for their transfer to a "better" class or by seriously considering such a possibility for them.[7] Arranging special help for the child by specialists, selecting him for participation in public events, such as school assembly programs, providing individualized supplementary work for him, and encouraging him to participate more in class are other kinds of teacher activity which aid the child to make greater progress in the school and perhaps eventually lead to a "better" class for him.

In addition to their selection for special academic attention, the least difficult children may be chosen for a variety of "help

[7]Fourteen of the "least difficult" children were actually transferred to a "better" class. Only four were placed in a "lower" class. These were all first-grade children who were members of a class that was completely disbanded after the school year began, with all of its members being assigned to other classes. The possibility of placing the child in a "better" class was spoken of in connection with an additional eleven "least difficult" children.

teacher" activities, including those whereby it is hoped they will
influence the social and academic behavior of other children. They
may deliberately be seated next to "troublemakers," or asked to
help other children with school routines and schoolwork. In some
cases, they may be placed in a position of controlling others' social
behavior.[8] Further incorporation of the child may occur as the
teacher defends or excuses actions which might be viewed as inex-
cusable in someone else, excepts the child when the rest of the
class is being punished, discusses any "problems" with him, tries to
get the support of other pupils and teachers for him, and in other
ways expresses particular concern for the child's welfare and progress in the school. The excerpts to follow reveal the variety and
extent of the beginning teachers' incorporation of some of their
pupils:

Second Week: I did say that Salvadore was not a problem. Now I'm not
sure if this is exactly true. His work is still very good. He is far ahead of the
rest of the class. . . . I did put him in the same desk [double seats] with
Ethel, thinking that he would possibly influence her. However, the influence has been just the reverse, and there has been a tendency to talk with
Ethel a great deal. Speaking to him now, he's not as cooperative. I'm going
to keep the seating arrangement for one or two more days and then see if
the effect is still the reverse. I will move Ethel somewhere else and possibly
put Lucy and Salvadore together so that the two of them can succeed.
However, I did want to put a good with a bad, thinking that possibly the
influence would be for the good.

Fourth Week: Salvadore Vasquez has been quite good. I mentioned last
week that because I had placed him in the same desk arrangement with
Ethel he was tending to become a little more talkative. He still is a little
talkative; however, he is concentrating on his work and is still able to do his
work quite well. He also finishes ahead of the children, but goes immediately to his more-to-do work and reminds Ethel that this is what she is to
be doing. He's usually quite eager to answer any questions that I put out.
He likes to be called on. . . .

The reading instructor and I were discussing Salvadore Vasquez. Although he has 125 I.Q. and seems to be quite bright in most areas, he is
only on the primer, but of course my children are on the pre-primer 1 and
2. Salvadore has finished the primer and is ready to move on to the next
book, so we're hoping that possibly we can put him in another class.

Fifth Week: I put Salvadore's name down as being misplaced or perhaps

[8]In the case of fifteen of the "least difficult" children, the beginning teachers mentioned that they were class officers. While class officers are usually elected by the
members of the class, the reports of some of the beginning teachers indicate that
teachers can influence these elections in various ways.

he would do better if he were in a more advanced class [on a recommendation form sent to teachers by the principal]. . . .

I have placed Salvadore and Raymond, the holdover, together. . . . Salvadore is doing a great deal with Raymond, especially in the line of reading. The two of them tend to finish the work, for example, rexograph sheets, alphabet work, or math work, before the other children—of course, Salvadore because I feel that he is a bright boy and Raymond because this beginning work he has had already, having been in the second grade. So I try to give them reading books, supplementary reading books, which the two of them work on together, and they seem very interested in reading together.

Sixth Week: When I spoke to the principal yesterday, she mentioned that Salvadore is definitely being transferred out. . . and that he's going to the top class of the second grade. . . .

* * * * *

When Roberta gets out of the classroom so much, when I give her so much freedom, she goes out in the hall, and she plays. Already three teachers have brought her back to me, telling me she's opening their doors. So now what I've done is I'm sending a monitor out with her—a good monitor, George. He takes her right to the door of the girls' bathroom and leaves her there, lets her go in, and waits for her to come out. If she doesn't come out right away, he comes and tells me. I had sent a girl with her, but she got the girl to play with her in there, so now I send a boy, and I'll see how that works out.

* * * * *

Two of my students, I'm very proud to say, are running for president and vice-president of the student government organization. One gets nothing but compliments. Every teacher that she has says that she is very reliable, a very responsible person. She is like a diamond shining like ice. She's really marvelous, very responsible. We're going to have a full-fledged campaign for her, and we're going to have little buttons, little stickers made, and I hope every child in my class will wear one.

In summary, the pupils whom teachers define as least difficult are those who conform to the officially required patterns of pupil activity in the classroom. These pupils reciprocate the professional efforts of teachers by devoting themselves to methodically performing the tasks assigned by the teacher. They recognize the authority of the teacher as one who knows more than they, and they accept the limitations on their own authority and competence. By adhering to the regulations and rules of the school, the least difficult pupils support the orderly procedures of the bureaucratic model for the teacher-pupil relationship and threaten neither teachers nor those who supervise them.

If all children in the slum school were like the least difficult children, the problem of "discipline" would not exist. Special problems arise in these schools, however, because many pupils do not share the values inherent in the bureaucratic model for the educational process. Unprepared for the requirements of the educational system and unsuccessful in the school, these pupils reject the efforts of teachers and fail to provide them with the response necessary to make them feel that their work is worthwhile. The dimensions of the problem and its consequences for the new teachers will become more evident as their accounts of the "most difficult" pupils are examined.

THE UNDISCIPLINED[9]

For the new teacher, encountering pupils who do not conform to the patterns of social behavior expected in the classroom is often professionally and personally traumatic. Unlike the good workers, these pupils nearly always fail to respond in ways that permit or enhance the professional work of teaching. On the contrary, the "most difficult" pupils typically cause teachers to spend an undue amount of time on what they feel is the "unprofessional" work of disciplining the child. These pupils, whom teachers sometimes describe as "on the borderline between good and evil" or as "bad," threaten both the authority of the teacher and the attainment of the educational goals of the classroom.

Teachers' complaints about pupils who violate the official norms of social conduct in the classroom are diverse. The emphasis is primarily on those aspects of pupil behavior which do not conform

[9]The data presented in this section are primarily based on an analysis of the elementary-school teachers' responses to Question 6 (see Appendix A), which asked each week that they describe their two or three most difficult children. The thirteen elementary-school teachers described a total of 175 children. Of these, half were mentioned over a period of five or more weeks. The number of most difficult children described represented 50 per cent or more of the total enrolled for three of the teachers and between 25 and 50 per cent for the remainder. In addition to the data provided by the responses to the specific question about their "most difficult" children, data on 56 additional children mentioned elsewhere as presenting problems of one type or another were also tabulated and are included in this discussion.

A similar type of analysis was attempted with the reports of junior-high-school teachers; however, they were not amenable to comparable tabulations. The junior-high-school teachers had many more children and several classes, and were therefore seldom able to give details about any one child over a period of time as were the elementary-school teachers. In the main, the patterns in the junior-high school are similar to those in the elementary schools, although the fact that the children are older and physically larger makes them more threatening to the teacher in some instances.

to the orderly procedures required by the educational bureaucracy. Hence, descriptions of the "most difficult" pupils are likely to include examples of disorderly behavior ranging from fidgeting or making faces to using obscene language or fighting. To a considerably lesser degree, teachers complain about the relationships of these pupils to other children, their social-psychological traits, and their scholastic characteristics. Only rarely does the teacher complain about the child's physical appearance or health.[10] Several types of complaints are illustrated by the following excerpts:

The second child with whom I have had the most difficulty is Henry Jenkins, who I have mentioned before. . . . I still have the same problem, that he daydreams. He just cannot seem to pay attention in class, and I have to interrupt a lesson so many times during the day because I realize that he isn't getting anything from it. He's not paying attention at all. He's just in another world, and I haven't made very much progress with him.

*   *   *   *   *

I had trouble with Roberto at the first of this week. He sits right in front of me . . . and he can talk to me. I'll be sitting at my desk, and he'll look over and take something from my desk. If I'm standing up and put something on my desk, he'll have to see what it is. He talks out constantly if I'm giving a lesson, without raising his hand, and he'll have the answers. He'll have wisecracks—like if I yell at someone to do something, he'll turn around and yell. I have my own little assistant teacher in there, and I keep saying, *"I'm* the teacher, not you. . . . Why are *you* telling them what to do?"

*   *   *   *   *

James is still presenting a problem to me. He has been quieter this week in that he has not been calling out as much, but he is quite immature for his age. Well, I guess not for his age, but he is more immature than the rest of the children in my class.

James has started a new thing. Everyday he raises his hand as soon as we get into class and asks if he can go to the bathroom. I have explained to them many times that they must go to the bathroom before they come to school, and I asked how many children did. James says he forgets. Sometimes I let him out and sometimes I don't. It depends how urgent his call seems to be.

The other day a funny incident happened. . . . I took the class to recess. Everyone was lined up except James. He was still in the bathroom. I went in, and I said, "James, are you almost ready?" He said, "I'm coming, I'm coming." The whole class was getting a bit restless just standing out in the hall. . . . Finally James came. . . . I said, "What were you doing in there so

[10]A list of the elementary-school teachers' complaints about pupils with whom they experienced difficulty is given in Appendix E.

long?" James said, "I had to make——" I won't say the word meaning to defecate. James thought this was a big joke that the whole class had to wait for him.

*　　　　*　　　　*　　　　*　　　　*

I believe I have mentioned in good part what has been happening with Larry Shaw's outbursts and acting out, etc. His work is practically at a minimum. He never brings a notebook to school or a pencil. Try as I will to encourage him or to give him work or to let him help me whenever possible, though it helps for a moment or so, there is really very little carryover. . . .

Last week there was an observer from the psychiatric clinic he attends. She comes in once every two weeks to observe Larry and Sammy in the classroom situation. . . . Either her presence in the class or something having to do with her completely upset him, and he refused to come out of the closet. He locked himself away, making silly sounds from the closet, threw down the other children's clothing, ripped the clothes. All of a sudden he ran out, ran up and down the aisles until he was shot in the head by a paper clip, which came from I don't know where. . . . and burst into a violent outburst of tears, ran up and down the hall disturbing not only myself but all the other teachers on the floor. He had some kind of whistle which he was blowing. . . .

*　　　　*　　　　*　　　　*　　　　*

I think the most important thing that happened in this school this week was . . . the trouble I'm having with some of my children. I've already told you about the occasion of swearing on the part of Ricardo Santos. I had sent him down to the principal for that, and since that he has been pretty good, much better than he had been.

This week, on Thursday, because it was Halloween, I was going to have a party. In the afternoon before my party got started I just happened to turn around, and I saw William Fields and Ricardo fighting again. I think I told you last week that they had a slight fistfight, nothing really serious, but this week as soon as I saw it, I saw blood coming out of Ricardo's lips, and I shouted for them to get into their seats, and it didn't work this time. I went and grabbed Ricardo, and I had to grab him with both hands because he's kind of big, and I just didn't think I was strong enough to hold him with one hand and while I'm holding him with both hands, his one hand was pretty free and he grabbed a chair and he wanted to swing it at William.

William had already gotten into his seat, and I was only afraid that I was going to get hit by the chair or William would get his eye knocked out or somebody else who would just happen to get in the way was going to get hurt. And all this time he was swearing and using obscene language again. I tried holding him and telling him to put the chair down. It didn't work, and finally I said, "If you don't put that chair down, I'm going to take you to the principal again." I sent one of the children for the teacher who is across the hall from me and she came in. I said, "Will you please stay with the class? I have to go down to the principal with a boy."

In the slum school, all teachers sometimes encounter pupils whose families have not taught them the behavior the school environment requires. There are other pupils whose inability to measure up to the standards in schoolwork means that they have not established a meaningful relationship to the formal curriculum. The new teachers often experience a sense of deep despair when they are assigned to such pupils:

Tuesday, it really was an impossible day for me. I just didn't know what I was going to do with Ron. I came home. I was hysterical. I cried all afternoon, all evening, and all night. I really felt that this was the end. I was not going back. What was the sense of knocking myself out for? It wasn't worth it. Here I was, trying to help people. They don't want to accept you, and this is exactly what I felt, very useless. I felt that I was not a teacher, that I was a policeman. What did I need this aggravation for?

   *   *   *   *   *

Once again, this was a week of disciplining the children. When I came back on Wednesday, they were very, very noisy. . . . Larry was in his glory then and still getting out of his seat. Irving Marshall was running all over the room, and Andy was running all over the place, and it was just a wild week. In fact, on Thursday they had me so upset that I went home crying, and I started to cry in the classroom. They just got me. Usually I would say, "I'm not going to let it bother me" and this and that. And it's just gotten to the point this week that . . . if they did just one more thing, I would just have sat down and started to cry. It was all I could do, and I was so mad that I slammed the door, and I just came out with the statement that if one person got out of his seat I would walk right out of the room. . . .

With all that discipline I naturally had not gotten beyond anything but the basic lesson—reading and arithmetic. We didn't do any art work this week—nothing. . . . If I threaten these children, they'll behave for about twenty minutes or so. Threatening, threatening, threatening is the only thing that penetrates. . . . I found out I am constantly threatening children, and you can't have a sensible lesson.

It took me all Friday afternoon to do a math lesson. One page took an hour. Why? Because they don't know how to open their books, and they don't know how to do the lesson. They have just become impossible. They talk all day, and while I'm yelling at them, explaining to them why they mustn't talk, they talk right in front of me unless I go over and pull on their arm or yell. If I turn around, they do it again, and honestly you don't know what to do after a while. . . .

I spend an average of two hours or more a day on discipline, getting them to work. . . . I have to stop every ten minutes to discipline them. I can't teach very much. I'm not there as a policeman but to try to teach them, and at the rate these children are going with disciplining, it's just impossible.

Usually, the activities, attitudes, and problems exhibited by the "most difficult" pupils are perceived by teachers as having no place in the classroom. Even the pupils themselves are sometimes considered as not belonging in the class. Faced with these pupils on a daily basis, teachers respond in a variety of ways. Essentially, they view their role as that of instilling the desired behavior in the child so that he may develop self-control, thus eliminating the need for the teacher to supervise anything except his academic work.

Both positive and negative sanctions are used in the attempt to make the child conform to the behavior expected by the educational system.[11] Positive sanctions include special rewards or help offered to the child. Negative sanctions may be as mild as a verbal reprimand or as severe as physical punishment or demotion.

In the case of those who persist in being obstreperous and fail to yield to teacher-imposed sanctions, the help of authorities outside of the classroom is enlisted. School principals, assistant principals, guidance counsellors, and the child's family constitute the core group to which the teacher turns for help, by means of letter-writing, conferences, or referral.[12] Usually the teacher evaluates the competence of these persons according to the support they give to the teacher's authoritative position and the improvement in the child's behavior.[13]

The teachers' efforts to control pupil behavior may be extensive and often require an enormous investment of energy and time. Yet there are some "difficult" pupils who respond negatively to these attempts and only remain alienated from the classroom or become more so. The following accounts of two difficult pupils over a period of several weeks will reveal how time-consuming these pupils can be and the range of approaches that may be used to control their behavior:

The Case of Carlos Sanchez

First Week: I had trouble all week with one child in my class. His name is Carlos. Now Carlos is a very slow child. He hardly does his work, and when he does do his work it is all wrong. . . . He took a pen and threw ink all over

[11] The reported ways in which the elementary-school teachers attempted to control the behavior of difficult pupils may be found in Appendix F.

[12] See Appendix G for a summary of the elementary-school teachers' use of authorities outside of the classroom for help with children who were discipline problems.

[13] See Howard S. Becker, "The Teacher in the Authority System of the Public School," *Journal of Educational Psychology, 27* (1953), 128–141.

one of the boy's shirts. He was fighting, and I understand that he caused trouble down in the yard. He was reported to me several times by the other teachers, and all in all he had been very trying all week long.

The principal brought him into the office along with me and yelled at the child and called up his mother while I was there. He warned the child that if he didn't behave, he would be expelled from the school. This seemed to have frightened the child. I hope not too much, but I hope enough so he will behave and do his work. I personally feel that if he really worked or tried to do his work, he would get along with the other children and be an asset to the class. I have decided to give him individual instruction and bring him up to at least the level of the class. . . .

Carlos, I found out, mimicked me. This is one thing I just can't take in a child. He was also quite disturbing in other respects. When I moved his seat and told him to do his work, he said to me, "I will not do my work because I don't like where I am sitting." This, I feel, is not the correct way for a child to behave.

He was isolated from the rest of the class because he started fighting with them. He took other people's pencils, he took their notebooks, he took their book covers. All in all, he was quite a disturbing child and at times obnoxious. When I was teaching a lesson, he would just sit there and laugh and giggle and make the rest of the class do the same. When I would ask him to come up to the board and do an example since he had nothing to do but laugh, I found out he didn't know a thing. I didn't know what to do with him until I realized that this child needed individual attention, and that's what he shall get. When the rest of the class is busy, I am going to take him aside and teach him individually, find out what his problems are. Maybe this way . . . he will be able to act as part of a class.

Second Week: Carlos holds the rest of the children back. He does not pay attention. He is a problem. I really feel he does not deserve to be in this class. . . .

This child is not a very clever child. He has a very bad family background. His mother is divorced, and he is one of five children. He is of Puerto Rican background, and no English whatsoever is spoken in the home. The thing is that this boy, more than anything else, needs attention. . . . I have tried to give him this attention, and I feel that he is coming along.

He is still a discipline problem, however, and I'm afraid he always will be because he has no self-control whatsoever. If he feels like whistling, he comes out and whistles. If he feels like stamping, he stamps. He does not, as yet, know how to control himself. The other day he went to the bathroom, and he stayed there for half an hour. He always leaves the room when there is a lesson going on. . . . I really feel this child is a guidance problem, and he is beyond my help.

I have given him individual help, and he seems to respond to it. I noticed lately that when we read the book, he shows me things in it. He is quite young for his age, but this can be because of his emotional problems. All he really wants is a little attention and a little help. I feel that, although he will always be a little difficult, maybe with more attention that he'll receive from me I'll have less trouble with him.

Fourth Week: Carlos is the same. . . . He still does not pay attention. He sits there eating candy. . . . The other day he was eating potato sticks, and I had him throw the bag away. While I was teaching the rest of the class, he went to the wastebasket and took the bag out. Of course, I had him throw the bag away, this time emptying it.

He tries to be the class clown, and the class laughs at him, but they get very annoyed because he is the cause of most of their trouble. When he says something wrong in the halls, the whole class is reported, and the principal has many times yelled at the whole class because of Carlos. To cite another example, he was making noise in assembly the other day, so one of the teachers yelled at the entire class. So, on the whole, the class is disturbed with him, and they don't like what is going on, as well as I don't.

I try giving him extra homework. I've tried giving him individual attention. I've tried helping him as much as I can, but nothing seems to be working right. So my best bet is to refer him to guidance. Maybe the psychologist can find the reasons for his behaving the way he does. . . .

. . . I will not allow Carlos or Manuel to be monitors. . . . I cannot teach a lesson with Carlos. He'll sit around. He'll start talking. He'll start making noises. Before you know it, I'll be yelling at him, and the children are sitting there bored because they don't know what to do. A good example of this was yesterday. I was teaching a lesson in punctuation. It got to the point where I couldn't take the child any more. I said, "Do you understand this?" He said, "No." So I explained. While I am explaining, he's turning around, looking out of the window, looking up at the ceiling, opening up a book to read. . . . I asked him to do the next problem, and he can't do it because he wasn't listening to what I was saying in the first place. So the windup was, I sent him out of the room. The children responded quickly, and they were so relieved that he had been removed. So, on the whole, the children feel as I do. He is definitely not an asset to the room. All he does is seem to cause trouble and make it difficult for everyone else to learn and to have a good time in class.

Fifth Week: The other day I was speaking to two other teachers about Carlos. He, I have just found out because it wasn't on his record, was in an Opportunity Class. An Opportunity Class is full of children who are discipline problems and learning problems. They do not know how to pay attention; they are supposedly the most difficult children in the school. Now I have Carlos, and I learned from these teachers that I could transfer him to another class.

This child, as is, is out of my class more than he is in it. He disrupts every single lesson. The other day I was giving a spelling lesson, and every other word he raised his hand to find out what the word was. This, of course, is an indication that he's much slower than the other children. Again we were doing a lesson in punctuation, and he was turning around and giggling and laughing and not paying attention at all. He always makes noises, and he is just impossible to cope with.

I find myself sending him to another teacher's room every day. There is just nothing I can do with him. And the other children are so disturbed about him because they want to learn, and he's always there to make things difficult for both me and the class, and I have to stop to discipline him at all times. So I was talking to Mrs. Taylor and Miss Schumann about this problem, and they told me that I can definitely transfer him and I should, either to a slower class or maybe back to the Opportunity Class. . . . I intend to write a letter to the principal telling him about Carlos, and also I have recommended him for guidance.

Sixth Week: The most important thing that happened to me in my school this week was that Carlos was transferred from my class into the Opportunity Class. As I said last week, last year he had been in an Opportunity Class, and he really did not belong in mine. . . . He did not do the work; he disrupted the entire proceedings. Just to cite an example, I was giving a spelling test on Friday, and after every word, I had to stop to reprimand him or discipline him. He did not have a pen, so he decided he didn't want to take the exam. So he just sat there, making noise and laughing and throwing things, getting up out of his seat, running around the room. He was just impossible for me to cope with.

So I went down to the principal during my lunch hour, and I spoke to him. I said to him that I could not cope with this child anymore. He did not belong in the class. He was disrupting the whole class. So the principal said that he was getting out. He said he definitely was putting him in the Opportunity Class where this child belonged in the first place.

As far as my feelings were concerned, for the class as a whole I was happy because I will have less interruptions, and I will be able to get through at least one lesson without having to stop to discipline him. As far as he himself is concerned, I must admit I feel very guilty because an Opportunity Class is not the best class for any child. He is a discipline problem, and this is a class made up of discipline problems. He needs individual assistance, of course. There are less children in this class, so maybe he will get this help.

I know, as I saw his reaction to the fact that he won't be in the class anymore, that he feels terrible. The children feel terrible, but I found he was suffering from this experience too. The children realize that he was impossible to handle. Anytime anyone did anything wrong, they were always blaming him. So although I feel guilty about having him transferred, maybe now he will be better off because he will be in a class with children who have the same problems. . . . Monday he will be put into the Opportunity Class. . . .

I did keep an anecdotal record on Carlos because he was getting on my nerves, and one of the teachers told me that this is the best way to get a child out of the class. Just in case they want proof of his behavior, I have it.

Thirteenth Week: The worst thing that has happened in my teaching career was the fact that I had to have Carlos transferred from my class. . . . No matter how I tried, I failed with him miserably. . . . To me, this was a personal failure because I could not deal with him and get through to him.

The Case of Gregory Bailey

Fourth Week: There are children that I am still having problems with. . . . One of these is Gregory Bailey. Just Gregory's appearance gives me the impression that there is something wrong with him. His eyes look quite heavy, and he sits with his cheeks puffed out and his eyes half-closed, and he has this arrogant expression on his face. He does not follow directions. He is slow. . . . He does poorly on his tests. He does not do his homework. . . . He will get out of his seat and go to the pencil sharpener or wash his hands when his row has not been called and he is not supposed to, and he knows he is not supposed to be out of his seat.

I've had trouble with him all along and what I've tried to do, of course, is reprimand him in class, shake him or scream at him. I've kept him in. I've given him extra homework. I've given him punishment homework—write "I must behave myself at all times" 200 times. I've given him his test papers to have signed by a parent at home, and this, of course, he has not done. I don't know whether he's afraid of his mother or he just doesn't remember to take the papers home, but he has not done this. I've also had him standing in the back of the room holding all his books, and I've also sent him to the kindergarten when he did not dress properly for auditorium or when he misbehaved. I really am not sure of what I am going to do next time he causes some disturbance in the class, but I do feel that I am going to have to send for his mother. Whether she will be cooperative or not, I do not know. I'm hoping that maybe she can influence him in some way.

Fifth Week: Gregory has been getting on my nerves also. He's constantly talking at his seat. He does not do his work. He doesn't start doing it on time, so he doesn't finish it on time. He doesn't finish copying his homework. He doesn't bother getting it from someone. . . . Even if he has copied his homework, he does not bother to do it. I think Thursday and Friday were the first two days that he ever did all of his homework. When he does it, he does pretty well.

He has also been taken out of line in the yard every day for talking on line and disrupting the class. This week I punished him by having him sit in a second-grade room. . . . After I had done this, I found out from the second-grade teacher that he had mutilated her bulletin board.

I had sent for his mother. We send a form letter down to be okayed by the principal, and then the mother comes in. I made an appointment for her for this week. I hope she shows up or answers my letter. If this does not work, I'm going to send Gregory to the guidance teacher. . . . She has spoken to him because she saw him one day in the hall, and she was disturbed at the condition of his eyes. He seems to have had an operation on his eyes. He was cross-eyed at one time, and he has something wrong with the muscles of his eyelids. So she has spoken to him about this condition, and I will send him down there one of these days when I cannot tolerate him any longer.

Sixth Week: I saw Gregory's mother on Thursday during my lunch hour, and I told her about his poor work, especially in arithmetic. I asked her if he had brought his papers home to be signed. . . . She said no, she never saw these papers. She wanted to know why he didn't bring books home. I told her because mostly the homework I give them I write on the board and they copy, and I use the books mostly in class for drill purposes. When he does have homework in books, of course, he should take his books home. At least twice a week he should take his social studies book home because I still give them homework in the book.

I also told her about his behavior, that he has been talking a great deal and getting out of his seat, and she said she would speak to him about this. She seemed cooperative, and I told her to make sure that he does his homework, to check his homework every night. I told her especially that he writes very slowly, and one of the reasons he doesn't have his homework every day is because he just never gets around to finish copying it. I asked her to try to light a fire underneath him to have him get his work done on time.

When I saw Gregory again in class that afternoon, I made him bring up his test envelope to get out his test papers for me to send home for his mother to see and sign, and I found that he had lost most of his test papers. I did find one arithmetic test that he had failed, and I sent this home with him. I said, "Have your mother sign it and bring it back tomorrow." He did not bring it back. He said his mother wanted to keep it at home, so I told him to please ask her to sign it and bring it back Monday. Now I'll see the cooperation I get on Monday and I hope that my speaking to his mother will improve his work and his behavior.

. . . I have started an anecdotal record on Gregory.

Fourteenth Week: Ricardo and Gregory are becoming actually obnoxious. They have not been doing their work. They both put a heading and number on their papers for math and spelling, but they do not write any of the words or the problems, so they both get zeros. They walk around the room, talk to each other, pick on other children, don't listen, don't copy their homework. They just are pretty much unmanageable and obnoxious.

I wanted to give them stars. I thought this would encourage them. I gave them stars one day when they tried a little hard to get on line, and it was good for just that one day. They were all right, but then they went back to their old pattern. They didn't even try for their stars, and when Gregory got a star, he just ripped it up. He didn't care. On Monday I'm going to send letters to their mothers saying that I want to see both mothers at the end of the week, because Gregory, after I had seen his mother the first time, was a little better. So I hope that now I'll see his mother again, he will improve again and Ricardo the same thing. So I'm going to send for their mothers again.

Sixteenth Week: The trouble with Gregory is that he does not seem interested in learning. He just does not want to do his work. I finally got

him to start copying his homework, so he has been doing half his homework, and, for instance, he did half the homework for Friday, so I made
him do the rest. I gave that to him as extra homework—punishment homework for Monday.

Another problem which I had with him was during reading when I was
working with the other group. He had an assignment, but I saw that he was
not doing it. He was sitting there reading library books from the public
library. Now I was thrilled to see that he had library books, and I went
over and I spoke to him about it. I said, "I'm very glad that you have
library books and that you want to read them, but if you would do your
work quickly and quietly and get done with it then you would have plenty
of time to read the library books and you wouldn't have to do them when
you are supposed to be doing other work." And this just didn't sink in, and
he went on reading library books until I had to take them away and make
him do his work. . . .

I sent for his parents before. . . and I had sent for them again. The
second time they never showed up, so I don't know what good it would do
for me to send for them again. . . . I'm going to have to speak to the
guidance counsellor during my free period on Monday about this problem
because I really haven't found a way to handle Gregory and interest him
in learning and doing his schoolwork. . . .

I think Melvin and Gregory also got the worst reports—again because
these two boys never do anything. All they do is cause trouble. . . . Gregory
could do fairly well. He could just get by if he tried, I think. But he doesn't
try at all.

Seventeenth Week: Most of the pupils are keeping up with the amount
and kind of work that I see as desirable for my class. The only ones that
aren't are Sally, George, Gregory, and Melvin. . . . And the only one of
those who I think is behind but making enough progress to feel that she
is among the working members of the class is Sally. The rest, I just sometimes feel that they are not among the live or working members of the
class. . . . I just don't think they are really participating meaningfully in
classroom work, and they are not getting anything out of it. . . . They do
participate sometimes. When they do, they participate meaningfully and
learn. But until they do, you can really die.

In contrast to the "least difficult" pupils, the "most difficult" ones
do not perform the activities which reciprocate the professional
and personal endeavours of teachers. Thus, they are unable to extend the professional image of what teaching and learning entail
and to make the progress in school which provides teachers with a
sense of satisfaction about their work in the classroom. They make
it difficult and sometimes impossible to teach, and they frequently
present a "hard core of resistance" that even highly motivated and
well-intentioned teachers may be unable to overcome despite many
attempts. The amount of time and effort required to cope with

these pupils may turn the teaching role into one of continually disciplining and policing pupils instead of instructing them.

Teachers would usually prefer not to have the "most difficult" pupils in their classrooms. Generally teachers come from cultural backgrounds in which formal education has been honored, and they themselves have worked hard to achieve success in school. They are unprepared for pupils who are alienated from the school and do not at least try to do their best to learn the skills and information which the teachers have been trained to teach. Although preparation and individual characteristics vary, most teachers have trouble with those pupils who seriously frustrate their instructional efforts.

The problems presented by the "most difficult" pupils from slum areas are too complex to be explained by the allegation that the basic difficulty is that the majority of teachers are white racists. Both Negro and white pupils are found among the "least difficult," as well as the "most difficult," and both Negro and white teachers have "most difficult" pupils who are Negroes. Those characteristics of difficult pupils which send teachers home in tears, evoke an array of usually ineffective and sometimes harshly punitive disciplinary techniques, and give teachers their worst days in the classroom have little to do with the skin color of either teachers or pupils. Rather, they have to do with the social behavior that fails to incorporate teachers into the roles they are trained to perform in the classroom.

When beginning teachers are unclaimed by those they teach, they feel lost in their new position of authority in the classroom. Their initiation into teaching is partial at best, and they often have a sense of failure with those pupils whom they are unable to reach. The "least difficult" pupils are frequently perceived as compensating for the "bad" ones, especially if there are enough of them; but even they may not fully make up for those who do not significantly participate in the classroom work initiated by the teacher. Similarly, the supportive help that parents and other adults may be able to give the newcomers does not necessarily completely allay the feeling of having failed to establish a meaningful teacher-pupil relationship with all in the classroom.

In the slum school, classroom relationships which incorporate both teachers and pupils into the work of formal education are often not established or maintained. The friction which arises when teachers meet difficult pupils, who are frequently recalcitrant, sometimes truculent, and nearly always strange to the ways of the school and its educational traditions, can and too often does turn the classroom into a battleground strewn with the educationally wounded. Both teachers and pupils may "die" in the process, as the classroom becomes a unit in a system of custodial care wherein the central teaching and learning function of the school is abandoned. When this occurs, the initiation of beginning teachers into significant roles of educational leadership in slum areas is truncated, even if they remain in the school. One of the consequences of this unhealthy situation is the way in which such teachers induct succeeding generations of newcomers into their roles in the school. The next chapter examines this particular consequence in detail.

5

THE CONSTANT GUIDES AND GUARDIANS

While it is true that most of the work of formal teaching in the contemporary school is done by individual teachers in physically separated classrooms, it is important to recognize the formal and informal work relationships which teachers have with each other. New teachers entering the school soon learn that they are not alone but part of a group of colleagues who attempt to guide and help them in many ways. Just as school administrators and specialists are anxious to induct the beginners formally into their new roles, so also are the other teachers eager to reach out informally and incorporate the new recruits into the group of teachers, and into one or more of the several cliques into which it is divided.

Beginning teachers' reports reveal that their relationships with older, more experienced teachers are highly significant and are not limited to joint work activities outside of the classroom, such as school assembly programs, gym activities, and patrol duties. Whereas the aid rendered new teachers by administrators and specialists, even if germane to the educational problems of the child, is spasmodic at best, experienced teachers are a constant source of help and guidance.

The new situation in which the novices find themselves has many facets for which they are not fully prepared. There are the problems of teaching formal subject matter to pupils who are behind in schoolwork and disciplining pupils whose social behavior does not conform to classroom norms. In addition, there is much to learn about the daily work routines of being a teacher and satisfying administrative requirements for plan books, classroom displays, and other bureaucratic procedures. Beyond the formal initiation by school administrators, colleagues instruct new teachers in these matters, thereby helping to shape and interpret to them the teacher's role in the school.

The informal induction by colleagues includes instruction in techniques of handling administrators and students and in the rules governing relationships with other teachers. Then too, new teachers learn from their colleagues the folklore of the school and its personnel, including students and the categories of students. Also important is the learning of how to evaluate and react to events in the school. As a consequence of these informal learnings, the new recruits develop a world view of educational categories and processes consistent with that of the other teachers in the school. Thus the details of teachers' groupings in the school and what is informally taught to the newcomers by the older teachers become highly important for an understanding of the socialization of the novices into their work.

THE INFORMAL TEACHER GROUPS

There are two types of informal relationships that new teachers have with others who teach in the school. One is primarily related to life outside of the school and is a grouping of those who are similar in age, length of time in the school, and interests. The second is related to the working of the educational system and brings together those who have common work problems and are seeking help from peers in solving them. The two kinds of informal contacts may overlap, but each has its importance in incorporating the new teacher.

The informal groupings of teachers according to similarities in age, sex, ethnicity, position in the school, and interests are most readily visible during the lunch hour, the one time during the school day when most teachers can get together.[1] The following

[1]In addition to the factors noted, lunchroom seating patterns may also be influenced by such things as the scheduling of more than one lunch period for teachers, the physical separation of one group of teachers and their classes in a separate building, and the choice of individual teachers to eat alone or in small groups outside of the school lunchroom.

excerpt describes some of the common groupings found in the junior-high-school cafeteria:

The informal groups of teachers in my school are rather interesting ones. I call one of them "the administration clique." This is composed of the assistant principal and some of the old-time teachers, not that they are old, but they have been in the school at least five or six years. When they have lunch during the fifth period, they are not kibitzing around or just gossiping idly as my group would be. They are discussing school policy or the problems of raising children in the suburbs. These people are in their late thirties or middle forties. . . . They are more responsible, and they are just more dedicated, if we can call it that, to work. They have many responsibilities. For instance, Mr. Gallo is in charge of the detention room. . . .

We have another group which I call "the segregated group." It is composed entirely of the shop teachers, the male deans, the health education teachers, and our music teacher. I'm always teasing them that no one can ever enter the solid areas of their table. They have two tables put together, and they just sit there and discuss shop or man talk. These are all men in their early thirties. Most of them have been married about five years. Some of them have one or two children or are expecting a child. They sit there, and they just discuss the things that men will discuss, or whistle at the girls as they pass by, or they will just sit there in their solemn dignity, and almost dare any woman to drop in on them. They are really loads of fun though. . . .

At the head table, or really the table nearest the kitchen area, is an all-female group. These are the women shop teachers, the sight-conservation teacher, one of the deans, the lady who has been in the school ever since it was built fourteen years ago, and occasionally Mrs. Lewin. These ladies have all been married fifteen to twenty years at least and have been in the school for quite a while, at least five to ten years. They usually discuss the problems of rearing grandchildren. . . . They are all very maternalistic toward me, and they will occasionally call me over and ask me how I'm doing or say that they like my new hairdo, especially on Mondays after I've gone to the beauty parlor Saturday afternoons. They are all very nice, but in a way they are aloof. Even if I have known many of these ladies for five to ten years, I would never consider calling them anything other than "Mrs. So and So." . . .

Toward the side is the noisy group, and yours truly is in that group. It's not that it's that noisy, but it's composed of about ten people who are young and perhaps a bit livelier than the other people. . . . Most of us have been in the school between one to three years, with the exception of Mr. Kirk and Miss Levy who have been there about three years for Miss Levy and about ten years for Mr. Kirk. Although Mr. Kirk is in his forties, he is very young in spirit and will usually stay with us. Although we will discuss the kids occasionally, as all teachers will, there is a different aura around the table. We will be discussing the latest books or anything current in the news or plans to go to the opera or movies. . . . I would say that the thing we most share in common is that we are all in our mid-twenties, fairly new at this school, and since most of the people are unmarried, we have this zest for going out a lot for parties and things like that.

In the elementary school, the informal lunchroom divisions among teachers are less diverse than in the junior-high school due to the smaller proportion of male teachers and lack of specialization in subject areas. Nevertheless, the social distinctions of age, sex, and position in the school play a major role in the formation of informal groups:

There are three long tables in the lunchroom, so there are three sub-groups. One group is the older women, the women in their forties and fifties, who are married, with children, and who have been teaching for years and years. A lot of these don't have one specific class. They're OTP, which means other teaching positions—people like the librarian, the read-ing teacher, the science coordinator, and various people. They sit together. They all bring in their diet food and their cottage cheese, and they have peaches. . . . This is the bulwark of the school—the older, stable teachers. They sit in their corner.
Then in the middle of the lunchroom are the young teachers, and this includes me. There's this long table, and it's sort of like segregation. One half of the table is the young teachers, and these are the new teachers who came this year. We sit around and we talk. Then at the other end of the table are some of the first-grade teachers and some of the teachers who have been there two or three years. They are young girls, and they play bridge.
The final table is the teachers who have been there maybe five or six years, but still the young ones—the young unmarried ones who are twenty-five to thirty-five. . . . This is sort of a flexible table because they come over to the other teachers' tables, and we sit and talk and everything. Of course, we go directly to our tables. Every now and then somebody will come over, and they will break the barrier and walk over to different tables to chat, but everybody has sort of an assigned seat, and when they walk in, they go right to these assigned seats. . . .
Then there is the other group that doesn't come to the cafeteria. These are the men. The men pretty much stick together because there aren't that many men teachers. They go out to eat, or they eat in one of the teacher's rooms. Then there is the group who are just women, and nobody gets to see them because they eat in their own rooms. They have a group, and I don't know who they are because I don't see them. . . . So all together I guess there are six subgroups.

From the above accounts, it is evident that patterns of social separation commonly exist in the school and that new teachers are somewhat socially isolated from the "old-timers" who occupy the most prestigious teaching positions.[2] The young teachers who have been in the school approximately one to three years, and are often still on probation themselves, are those with whom the beginners have the most informal contacts of a social nature. Frequently these contacts are concerned not with school activities but with social events outside of school hours. These range from weekend dating activities and vacationing to simply going to a friend's house after school or riding to and from school together in a car pool or on the same public transportation.[3]

In contrast to the informal contacts of a social nature, those which are based on work problems usually involve the "old-timers." Frequently an experienced teacher has a special relationship to the beginner by virtue of having been his or her cooperating teacher during student teaching, having previously taught the pupils now assigned to the beginner, or being formally assigned a "buddy teacher" or grade leader. Sometimes, however, an experienced teacher is simply interested in helping the new teachers along and becomes what one teacher aptly describes as "a constant guide and guardian." Through such contacts the beginning teachers learn how to present themselves as competent and efficient professional workers in the school who will cherish and guard the traditional relationships with both pupils and administrators.

THE TEACHER AS MANAGER

Teachers are not only supervised by those in positions above them; they are also expected to manage and supervise those in positions below them. Their management role has many facets. It includes the teaching of subject matter and technical skills to subordinate pupils, the provision of an attractive work setting in the classroom, the planning of lessons, and attendance at conferences and meetings with supervisors, specialists, parents, and others.

[2]All twenty-two teachers report that the "old-timers" form a subgroup within their schools. The segregation of males is common, and five of the teachers (representing three schools) noted that the Negro teachers in their schools ate alone.

[3]There is wide variation in the extent to which the twenty-two teachers participated in social activities outside of school hours with other teachers in the school. In general, this type of activity is not reported by married teachers or by most of the engaged teachers. For the single teachers and a few of the engaged teachers, however, it plays a greater role. The double-dating reported is usually that in which the female teachers introduce friends they have made in school to members of the opposite sex whom they have met outside of school. Among elementary-school teachers, particularly, the social activities outside of school are sometimes limited to a teacher friend whom one has known in college or high school.

Even more importantly, it involves controlling the behavior of pupils in such a way that they perform their work tasks in an orderly manner acceptable to the school system.

Learning to manage efficiently the many tasks assigned to them is not easy for beginning teachers. Like new workers in all work settings, they are largely dependent on their more experienced colleagues to teach them the procedures for coping with the demands made upon them by their supervisors and subordinates which have evolved out of long experience. A summary of the types of help in management given the beginners by the older teachers will begin to indicate the important role of the more experienced teachers in the socialization of the novices. This aid is primarily directed toward the establishment of work routines, the teaching of subject matter, the provision of educational tools and classroom displays, the preparation of plan books, and the filling out of class records.

One of the common difficulties experienced by the beginning teachers is to guide pupils in making the transition to schoolwork activities after they have been engaged in other activities. Usually such transitions are necessary after periods when control by teachers has been more relaxed than usual or completely lacking; for example, at the beginning of the morning and afternoon sessions after pupils have been away from the classroom for relatively long periods and following a short recess or a time of passing from one classroom to another.

Following these periods of attenuation or lapse in the formal patterns of classroom relationships, experienced teachers employ several techniques to re-establish their authoritative position, the subordinate roles of pupils, and the atmosphere of quiet in the classroom so that educational work may proceed. By means of these procedures, the experienced teacher regains control of the class and is often free to attend to clerical work before beginning a series of actions concerned with the teaching of the formal lessons of the day. A sampling of these techniques is provided by the following quotations from beginning teachers' reports:[4]

The most important thing I have learned was from Ann Goldsmith, who puts herself into your position when you speak about anything that goes on in the classroom. She explained to me certain things that I would have to

[4]Although only four teachers report specific techniques given to them by other teachers for beginning class sessions, the types of techniques described are in common usage in the schools in which the teachers taught, and others tell of using them.

do in order to control the class better. She suggested that in the morning when I come in I should write an assignment on the board for them, one that would take approximately one half hour so I could get all my clerical work done and keep them busy at the same time. Do the same thing at 1:00 when we return from lunch, but make that a fifteen-minute assignment where the children will be kept busy while I would be able to do my clerical work. This, I feel, is invaluable. It was just a fantastic idea, and this is what I am doing now, and it does eliminate much of the noise, and it's understandable, because the children are now occupied.

*   *   *   *   *

I have been told by several math teachers that the first thing to do is to have work for them on the board and just settle them down. This I will do for about ten or fifteen minutes of the period. As they are working, I usually go around the room, and I check the work, or if they have questions, I answer them individually.

*   *   *   *   *

The most important thing that happened to me in my school this week was speaking to Mr. White. . . . Mr. White is a teacher who has been teaching English for about nine or ten years. . . . He saw that I was a little bit down in the dumps while I was patrolling the halls. . . . He stopped me to ask how it was going, and I told him I was having trouble with the discipline in some of my classes . . . that I was having a hard time getting control of the class, and that I was teaching out of license.

He suggested that for this week, I treat them as a slow class rather than as a bright or average class and give them constant drill work and use my voice in the classroom as little as possible. He suggested that when they come into the room I should have the "Do Now" on the board, even though I don't have control of class. On the right side of the board, I should have just a heading, "Those Not Working" and another heading "Those Going on the Section Sheet."[5] I should just point to it when they get to their seats and pray that they'll calm down, and I should just start to walk around the room while they are doing this "Do Now" and start marking people down on the blackboard. He suggested that I reverse the lessons around and have them fill in, have them spell spelling words right, have them copy them over, and expose myself at the front of the classroom as little as possible until I gain a little more confidence in myself.

Afterwards, he said this is about all that he could suggest for now, that this should work, that it worked about 80 per cent of the time. . . . I really felt good after talking to Mr. White. A little of the knot in my stomach eased up.

[5]A section sheet is a form given to junior-high-school classes by their homeroom teachers at the beginning of the day. Some member of the class is responsible for turning it over to each subject teacher during the course of the day. The subject teachers comment on the behavior of the class and report any pupils who have misbehaved. The section sheet is finally returned to the homeroom teacher, who takes appropriate action.

A second set of problems typically encountered by new teachers concerns the presentation of the formal curriculum. The techniques of teaching subject matter, the use of appropriate teaching materials, the preparation and writing up of formal lesson plans, and the classroom display are matters about which the beginners often feel uncertain. By means of the informal exchange of ideas, directly seeking or receiving the advice of those more experienced, and informal observation of what others do, the new teachers typically receive a good deal of aid:[6]

I see Sam Jones quite often during my free periods when I patrol, and I have taken home his lesson plan books from last year for seventh grade. He teaches social studies, and I wanted to see how he broke down the curriculum. . . . I checked his plan book for social studies at the beginning of the term a few times, and copied a few of his lessons. Boris Seymour, who is also teaching out of license, and Sally Zukoff have borrowed my English plan book at times to copy some of my lesson plans.

*   *   *   *   *

There's a teacher, Mrs. Bailey, who is the one that told me what to do about division because she saw that the children didn't understand it. She's very nice. I have one of her plan books as sort of a guide for me. . . . She told me anytime I need help, I should just come to her. . . .

*   *   *   *   *

Mrs. Leone, who is the teacher in the room on one side of me, has given me several ideas about the setup of lessons, especially working on the calendar, the type of calendar to use, how to use it. . . .

*   *   *   *   *

Mr. Lerner has been very helpful in telling me how to work with a slow class. You only take one point, and you hammer it home one period, and then you go over it the next day, and you keep going over it as you are teaching something new. You go very slowly, to feel out the class, to see what they are like. . . because you have to remember that they are not getting whatever you are saying if you are giving them too much. Don't give them too much.

[6] All of the teachers report specific instances of receiving help with these matters, and nearly all of them were given help, especially with materials to use in teaching and the presentation of subject matter. Because the majority of children in the slum school are behind in schoolwork and the schools themselves have difficulty obtaining adequate teaching materials for children with these characteristics, the beginning teachers experience particular problems in knowing what to teach, how to teach it, and what teaching aids to use. As noted earlier, the writing of plan books is something new teachers learn quickly, and in some instances they receive plan books prepared by experienced teachers directly from school administrators. Hence the need for help with this problem is usually not acute. Room decorations and displays are easily observed, and few teachers report going to other teachers for help with this problem.

*   *   *   *   *

I've learned quite a bit about bulletin boards from Mr. Panetta. He has his whole back bulletin board covered with *Time* magazine covers of famous people, and then he has John Hancock material and maps that he has hung up in his room. So he gave me some supplies, some things he had torn out from the newspaper. . . . He was in a few times to help me, and another teacher was there yesterday when I was decorating.

In addition to advice and guidance in "settling the class down" and presenting the curriculum, the older teachers provide help in doing clerical work efficiently. For new teachers this work can be especially burdensome because of the variety and number of records to be kept and the fact that they are unfamiliar. Accounts from two teachers reveal the complexities involved, as well as the extended help some of the older teachers give:

Mr. Danna, with whom I'm sharing my official room, has been a tremendous help this week. He was my cooperating teacher last term when I student taught at this school. He's explained all the little details, such as attendance cards, and how they are made up, and when they are due.

They also have a special attendance report which is a sheet of paper, and all they care about are numbers—the register, the present register, the register that you had the day before, the number of people absent, the number of people admitted without instruction. I think "without instruction" means that they have not been in school so far this year, and you have to enter the number there. . . . It's just every day you have to fill this in—the numbers. He's helped me with that because it was a little hazy at first—how you knew what your register was or what would happen if someone would come in at the middle of the day.

*   *   *   *   *

Today at school we had Health Week. We had two free periods in the morning for that. I say "free period"—I had my class, but I gave them busy work to do so I could fill out these forms. One of the teachers, Miss Barrett, came in and helped me. She was very helpful. It would have stretched out to four, five, or six periods because I really didn't know what to do. I wasn't given much instruction. As usual I was handed a page of print, two pages —long pages of printed matter—and told to read it. There were so many things to do, and I didn't know how to go about it or how to do it. Fortunately for me, Miss Barrett came in, and within a period she had everything answered and knew just exactly what to do, and it went so quickly. If it hadn't been for Miss Barrett, I would have been working on it probably all day and all the following day, and I probably still wouldn't have it done.

As those expected to manage classes in slum schools, new teachers face special problems. There are the difficulties of teaching the formally assigned content to the child who is behind in schoolwork. These difficulties are frequently exacerbated by lack of adequate and appropriate teaching tools. Even greater perplexities are presented by the social behavior of many pupils. By constantly supporting the position of the teachers in the school and training the newcomers in attitudes and procedures congruent with an image of the teacher as one who is in charge of the class and whose orders are to be followed by pupils, the experienced teachers transmit to the new generation the behavioral patterns which continue the tradition of the teacher as the central and most important figure in the school, whose authority must not be undermined if the work of formal education is to be done. The details of this part of the beginners' induction by the older teachers will be discussed next.

The Teacher as Disciplinarian

The older teachers in the school have knowledge about the classes and many of the individuals within them. They also know the rating of classes and individuals according to the criteria of ability and social behavior. In some cases, this is direct knowledge on the part of those who have taught particular classes and students in the past. In other cases, a class or an individual has acquired a reputation which other teachers have heard about. Very early in their teaching career, and sometimes dating back to the days of student teaching in the same school, new teachers learn about the reputation of their classes. Often they solicit or are voluntarily offered information from those who have taught them, and they nearly always receive written records about the individual pupils in their classes. The teacher grapevine and the written records kept by former teachers play an important part in the formation of the beginning teachers' anticipations about those whom they teach. Among the new recruits to the slum school, the usual effect is to lower initial expectations. The following excerpts from a teacher assigned to the bottom class on her grade reflect a pattern which, although not as boldly present in other situations, is nonetheless typical of general attitudes among the experienced teachers toward many classes in the school.[7]

[7]Only one of the elementary teachers gives a report indicating she was frequently and consistently told by the other teachers that she had a "good" class. The remainder of the elementary teachers were either told that they had "bad" classes or specifically warned about "troublemakers" in the class. Among the junior-high-school teachers who taught several classes there was greater variety, since their various classes had different reputations.

First Week: The older teachers who have been there three or four years usually sit together. Yesterday I had yard duty, which meant I had to eat lunch a little earlier than the rest of the teachers, so I ate with two of the older teachers. . . . We discussed some of the idealism behind teaching. I was told they wouldn't advise someone to come into the school system. When I asked the reason, they told me that the children were getting to be too hard to handle. . . . They also told me how in a couple of weeks my idealism would have been worn off. It's easy to work with a slow class that is well behaved because you don't have to work too hard. I should not expect too much from these children whose I.Q.'s are in the high 60's and low 70's, and I should just try to teach them as much as I could. . . .

I was assigned a buddy teacher who has been a lot of help to me. He and my supervisor warned me about this boy, Robert Moore. So far I haven't had too much trouble from him, but I was told that he has an unhappy home life. . . . Mostly I have learned about some of my children from other teachers.

Fourth Week: Mrs. Holtzman was a teacher last term, and now she's the library teacher. She usually takes my class if I have yard duty or a conference. . . . She told me, "I feel sorry for you having those kids for the whole term because they're a wild group." . . .

There's a teacher whose line is always behind me. . . . She's an experienced teacher. I don't know how long she's been teaching, but she's another one who reassures me that I'm doing well, and I have a bad class, and I have to make the best of it.

Fifth Week: I got a note from the teacher who taught Larry last year, and it says, "Larry is very self-conscious about being short, and you have to compliment him and make him feel like a big man in front of the class." . . .

Mrs. Lanier is the reading teacher, and lately she's been praising me so much that I don't understand it, mainly because I don't think the praise is deserved. . . . We walked into the teacher's room, and she brings me over to the table with the old teachers and starts saying, "This girl is just terrific. She's doing such a marvelous job. Do you know what she does for social studies? She takes the textbooks home, and she writes over the paragraphs." . . . Then an older teacher started in telling me that soon I would start getting letters with four letter words. The kids start writing letters to the teachers using obscenities, and I shouldn't be surprised when I get these and think they are sending them just to me, because the older teachers get them.

And there's another teacher, Phoebe Epstein, who teaches the last fifth grade on the grade. She's a lot of help to me because she encourages me. . . . We have yard duty together, and we talk. And I always say, "I just don't know what I'm going to do. I can't seem to cover anything during the day. I just do reading and arithmetic, and that's all I get to cover during the day." She encourages me. She's really terrific. She tells me, "Just do what you can; don't be disappointed. Everybody has the same thing. It's not only you." She starts telling me about the things to do in my class, and she gives me a feeling that I'm not the only one who's going through this. She's been teaching for seven years, and she helps me a lot.

Sixth Week: Miss Howe, who is in charge of the intellectually-gifted class on my grade and one of the experienced teachers, expressed an opinion that she didn't like my class. She didn't like their faces.

In the above account, several aspects of the induction by the more experienced teachers are apparent. There is first the training of the recruit in an ideology about her pupils which emphasizes their "bad" characteristics. Secondly, there are the words of advice about not expecting too much of the pupils in terms of schoolwork and the observation that the teacher of the "slow class" does not have to work too hard because of the scholastic limitations of the pupils. Finally, there is the psychological support of being told that one's failure and disappointments about progress in the classroom are shared by others and are largely the result of the characteristics of the class to which one has been assigned:

I feel a little better from these discussions with the more experienced teachers in that I'm still having trouble with the days of the week. But Miss Croyter and Mrs. Brown said that they really don't learn it at all, and that it's just a drudge for the whole time. Miss Croyter said her class last year didn't know the days of the week until maybe the last day of school.

New teachers often learn that they are not expected to achieve as much scholastically with their assigned classes as they might be if the children had better academic abilities, but they also learn that they must establish and maintain control over the pupils. Pupils in these schools are viewed as lacking in self-control and therefore in need of being controlled by the teacher until they learn to respond in the orderly manner demanded by the school.[8] Many discipline techniques are suggested to the beginners so that this may be achieved:[9]

[8]This rationale is not peculiar to schools in the slum. See Frankie Beth Nelson, *"Beginning Teachers' Induction into the Social System of an Elementary School."* Unpublished Ed.D. dissertation, Teachers College, Columbia University, 1962.

[9]The excerpts quoted are from six different teachers. The majority of teachers report similar approaches to discipline on the part of the old-timers. The following instance of advice given to a junior-high-school teacher is the only one of its kind reported by the teachers in this sample: "Miss Caplovitz, a teacher that I formerly had, . . . told me that to be a teacher was one of the most wonderful things in the world, and that she was very proud of me, proud of the fact that I had chosen teaching as my profession. She also told me something that she had learned about teaching, that a good teacher never raises her voice, and the good teacher never uses the section sheet against the class, which I too felt was true. You must always talk to them as you would talk to an adult, and you must never talk or scream at

I've had the most interaction with a teacher named Marion Agronsky. This is her second year of teaching, and she said that last year she had a great deal of problems with her students. She couldn't handle them. . . but after a whole year of coping with her children, she feels that now she has the equipment to stay on, and she is accepted as a good teacher in my school. I was talking to her this week, and she was so helpful to me, more helpful than anyone else I think.

She told me exactly what her routines are, exactly how she organizes things, and she told me that I can step into her room any time I want to and just sit in the back and observe her. I took her up on this, and I could tell you some of the methods she uses to get control and catch the interest of the students.

This is the second week of school, and she hasn't started anything in her subject area, which is social studies. She hasn't taught the children anything yet. She has them write down the rules for routines for lining up, for entering the room, for standing and facing the class. She has them review it. She has them practice it over and over and over again. She does this, writing down, reviewing it, practicing it until this is coming out of the children's ears. She has wonderful control of the children, and she does have difficult classes to begin with, but the control is very, very good, and she expects to be teaching soon. But she says that anyhow she can't teach without establishing these routines, . . . and this is what she advises me to do. . . .

She gave me other tips about treating children. She told me to write letters home for any disturbances immediately, and I have my letters written now which I will mail either today or tomorrow. She said this is very effective. . . . When students continue to act up, I should call for their parents to come in to school. She also told me not to be afraid to fail any child who acts up or doesn't do his work, and anything you say in class must be followed up.

> *   *   *   *   *

From one teacher over the lunch table I did learn one discipline measure. He said it was unfortunate that I did not wear a college ring for he found, turning the ring about, the stone on the palm side of his hand was very good discipline when making contact with the back of a student's head. It seems to leave them somewhat stunned for the moment and somewhat mindful that they should behave. Though I intend to use persuasion rather than physical violence, I did think that this piece of discipline information was useful.

> *   *   *   *   *

I spoke to Miss Wiener during my teacher preparation period in the lounge about discipline. She again reminded me to be firm and to scare

---

them because this makes them scream back, and it makes them just as rebellious as they were before."

them and make them fear you so you will have no trouble with them later
on.

*   *   *   *   *

The teacher in the room next to mine has been in this school several
years. She uses something very effectively to keep children from talking
and using filthy language, which is a great problem in our school. Get a
soap dish and make the children take a lick of the soap every time they talk
whenever they are not supposed to or use a word they shouldn't. This is
very effective. I don't know how the Board of Ed. would smile or frown on
it, but it was effective, and it was instantly effective.

*   *   *   *   *

I told Miss Lerner that I got rid of Sammy. It just so happened that she
had him for a little while before he was put into the Opportunity Class in
the fourth grade, and she knew what he was like. She was one of the
teachers who told me to try to get rid of him. I did speak to Miss Morris
and also to Mrs. Feldman, and both of them told me to make anecdotal
records about this child. They also told me how to do it. They said to look
up his record, and the best thing to do was to obtain so much information
about him that I would be able to get rid of him.

I also found out that Miss Morris had one of my other students, Robert.
She said that he is emotionally disturbed and quite a problem. She said
. . . that one day she had stepped out of the room. When she came back,
he was lifting a chair to hit another child over the head. Well, she knocked
his hand in such a way so that the chair would fall over. The chair bounced
up and hit him in the nose, and his nose started to bleed. Since this time,
she didn't have any more trouble with him. Of course, this is something I
can't do with him, but I find that as long as I show him who is boss and
not let him get away with anything I can handle Robert.

*   *   *   *   *

The other teachers have all stopped and given me little clues as to how
to control the class. For instance, the kids were rather noisy at dismissal
time, and they weren't going down the same staircase. Some were jumping
over the bannisters, and they were just not going down like human beings,
so one of the teachers whom I had worked with last year told me that the
best way to control them is to stop after each landing and just wait for
silence. If I don't get it, say, "John is holding up the class. As soon as he's
quiet, we'll go down." This way, there will be pressure from the rest of the
group, and the kids don't like this. They don't like to be "in bad," as the
saying goes, with the rest of their classmates. . . . This was a very good hint,
and just applying it once showed me that it was a valuable hint. As I say,
I'm really grateful to those teachers. Most of them have been teaching
between two and five years, something like that, so they still remember the
experience of just starting, . . . being found with thirty kids and just dying
right there in front of the room, not knowing what to do.

Other teachers regard the teacher of each class responsible for the training of his or her children, and children who misbehave in the school while they are not with their homeroom teachers are reported to them. New teachers are carefully watched by both the older teachers and school administrators to see if they have established control:

Once in a while someone will stop me and say, "Your class is very good. Really they are doing quite well," or someone will say, "Oh, your class, the boys today were just so terrible."

These factors, together with the special problems posed by the children of the urban poor, often combine to give the new teacher the feeling that her task is largely one of disciplining, to an extent which interferes with teaching as much as she would like. As a consequence, feelings of discouragement overtake many new teachers, who then may be supported by the more experienced:

I felt so discouraged when I couldn't seem to get them quieted, and I said to myself, "Miss Visertini said she couldn't let down until Christmas." So I figure I still have a month, practically two months to go. So maybe by Christmas I will have them in order and completely quiet. . . . We shall see what happens, but it's pretty rugged.

Thus far, the focus of the discussion has been on attitudes toward the child which perpetuate the tradition of the teacher as the most important figure in the school. Yet the child is not the only potential threat to the teacher; administrators may also challenge what teachers think of as their proper role and territory. In what follows it will be seen that in this problem also the older teachers are constant guides and guardians of what the relationship between the beginners and their supervisors should be.

Teachers United

The main thrust of the older teachers' induction of the new teachers is related to their role as managers and evaluators of children. However, teachers also evaluate administrators and supervisors and have tested ways of controlling them. At times special events evoke strong support for the beginners and the older teachers act against the administrators on their behalf. In addition, the beginners turn to the more experienced teachers for advice on the management of lessons being observed by the supervisory staff. The following reports reveal some of the support given to beginners so that they may better control their supervisors:

I told some of the teachers about what had happened Friday, with the principal walking into the classroom, taking over the class, and sort of telling me what was wrong with my room right in front of the children. The teachers were very upset, and said that I should speak to him. This I did, but not on Friday.

*   *   *   *   *

I have also been interacting with the teachers this fall about the problem of Phillip, because they were all very upset about his behavior in the assembly and they all felt he should be suspended or some disciplinary measure should be taken. I know I myself really didn't say anything to the assistant principal, and she found out. Quite a few of the other teachers, for my sake, went to speak to her, to tell her that they didn't think that it was fair that I should more or less have this burden placed upon me, because they saw how difficult it was to cope with him because they themselves, who were experienced teachers, couldn't get anywhere with him, and the reading specialist had her difficulties with him, as did the guidance counsellor. They didn't feel I should be taxed with such a problem. I found out about this, and their concern for me was quite a nice thing, so that it really made me feel that the other teachers are on my side and they are really working for you and in your best interests. This is very good.

*   *   *   *   *

I spoke to another sixth-grade teacher. She told me certain things that the principal would look for when he came in to observe me. She said, for example, that he likes the teacher to call on children to evaluate each other's answers. For example, if I were to call on Jimmy, and he would answer, I should call on another one and ask that pupil what he thought of Jimmy's answer. She also told me that the principal likes to take over in the middle of the lesson. And she told me that he really didn't know very much about reading, so it really didn't pay to do a reading lesson, but that he likes to see social studies, and he also likes to see some routines.

*   *   *   *   *

I went to talk to Mrs. Schorr, who told me of the many incidents that she had with the assistant principal. She told me not to worry, that very few people could get along with her, and that if I let her get on my nerves it would be just terrible. She told me to avoid her and disregard what she told me about initiative and growing up because it was uncalled for and she talks to everyone that way.

The mutual support of teachers in the face of administrative requirements, the idiosyncrasies of particular administrators, and threats to their authority is most visible in the union movement among teachers. New teachers are approached early to join the union, and many of them choose to do so. A few even become active in union activities during the first semester and accept leadership roles. The exclusion of administrators from the union further extends the claiming of the teacher by a colleague group, quite distinct from the supervisory group.

The U.F.T. in my school is very strong. As a matter of fact, our chapter chairman had mentioned that it was one of the strongest in any of the junior-high schools in this city. Practically everyone in school belongs to it. I joined the union last year after having been involved with the union more or less for a long time. I must clarify this by saying that one of my best friends is one of the vice-presidents of the union. I have known him for ten years, so naturally all these years I have been bombarded with pro-U.F.T. propaganda, if that's the word for it.

I felt that I had to join, not only because I believe in its principles—and I do think they are worthwhile—but whether I join or not I will be affected by the union. So as far as I was concerned, . . . if I could have a voice in it I felt it would be much better. . . .

Another point that has come up was that some of the administrators had asked that the principal group be affiliated with the U.F.T. One of our delegates to the union asked that we vote against this when it comes up. We all chipped in a dollar so that we can put an advertisement in the newspaper asking that people vote against it. As the delegate said, "No administrator has ever walked out with us when we have gone on strike. They make more money than we do. They are not in sympathy with our ideals, so frankly why should they be involved with us and why should they get the benefit of anything we do?"

The highlights of new teachers' informal initiation into the school by the older, more experienced teachers have now been described. These guardians of the traditional definition of the teacher as the most important person in the school emphasize that the teaching group is separate and distinct from the administrators and the pupils. They impress upon the new recruits the need for tight control of subordinate pupils and the protection of the classroom from unwarranted invasion by superordinate administrators. Gradually they incorporate the beginners into the group and train them in the behavior, values, and attitudes which they define as appropriate for those who are teachers in the educational bureaucracy.

In the slum school, the informal incorporation into the teaching corps often has unanticipated consequences for the practice of teaching in the classroom. Those things that are learned by the beginners from the teachers who have been in the school some time are seldom related to the special function of the school in poverty-stricken areas or to the educational needs of children whose social and cultural backgrounds are quite different from those to which teachers are accustomed. On the contrary, the experienced teachers stress traditional bureaucratic categories for evaluating and classifying pupils and their behavior and a definition of the teacher's role which does not include active involvement in the community surrounding the school.

Most beginning teachers in the slum school experience considerable anxiety about what to do in their new situation. They voice many fears about losing control of the class and failing to teach the information and skills prescribed by the formal curriculum. Personal inadequacies, professional ineptitude, inexperience, and students who do not respond to their work and challenge their authority and professional abilities contribute to the newcomers' uncertainties and apprehensions.

The experienced teachers are sensitive to the beginners' feelings of frustration and despair, of being lost or "dying" in front of the class. They reach out to them and offer remedies to help them through the hard periods. These solutions are basically congruent with the formal initiation given by supervisors, although they sometimes include practices designed to help teachers meet bureaucratic demands which would not be approved by administrators. The solutions offered by the old-timers stress the importance of keeping pupils quietly occupied and forcing them to respond to the activities of teachers, even if several days, weeks, or months are required to drill them in the routines of acting out their subordinate role in the classroom. The common belief is that teachers can teach and pupils can learn only when pupil-initiated activities, toward other pupils and the teacher, are stopped. Those pupils who do not sit silently at their desks, listen to what teachers say, and do the work assigned to them not only cannot be taught but do not deserve to be.

Such beliefs about the teaching and learning process provide an ideology which allows teachers in the slum school to maintain a professional identity even when they fail to teach pupils in ways that enable them to achieve in the educational system. The inability to gain control of pupils or to engage them in meaningful educational activities can be a personally and professionally devastating experience. It is much less so if one ascribes the fault to the traits of pupils and their parents and to administrators who fail to provide the support needed for teaching success, and if one receives strong support for this perception from older colleagues.

This induction of new teachers which reiterates the essence of customary bureaucratic classifications and approaches to pupil behavior at best trains them to carry out traditional teaching procedures among the "least difficult" pupils. At worst, they learn to play a solely custodial role in relation to the "most difficult" pupils. In the latter case, the first year of teaching largely becomes an experience of serving time until one has been in the school long enough to be assigned a better class or can leave the school altogether to work in a more desirable situation. Even at best, the older teachers' induction of the beginners into their new position often alienates them from those they teach and leaves the newcomers unclaimed by pupils and their parents. When this occurs, both new and old teachers are viewed by many in the communities they serve as those who, having abandoned the task of educating the children of the poor, are no longer worthy of a professional role in the school.

6

TEACHERS IN CRISIS

Upon entering the slum school, new teachers are inducted into an educational system that inhibits the learning process for most pupils in the school. Throughout their formal preparation, teachers are trained to respect, nurture, and advance the central goals of the educational system by socializing the young for roles as adult participants in our society. Yet, there is growing evidence that teachers are failing to adequately prepare the child for the world in which he will live as an adult, or for any world except that in which he now lives. The general extent of the failure is unknown, but there can no longer be any doubt that it is acute and widespread in schools attended by large numbers of pupils whose families are members of the lower social classes in our society.

New teachers who undertake professional work in schools located in urban slums are quickly socialized into activities and ways of thinking which perpetuate the dichotomy which exists in all schools between the adult professional staff and the child-pupil clientele. In these schools this dichotomy has reached extreme proportions, and teacher-pupil relationships often make a mockery of ideal textbook versions of how teachers do and should behave. The past experiences of teachers in classrooms, even those intended to prepare them to teach, fail to provide useful models for engaging pupils in educational work. Neither do supervisors provide teachers with a model for achieving professional success among pupils whose own past experiences in home, neighborhood, and school have frequently not equipped them with a model of the social and academic responses teachers expect.

120

Both the formal preparation for teaching and the formal curriculum prescribed by the school emphasize the role of the teacher
as one who transmits knowledge and academic skills to pupils.
Teachers are expected to train pupils throughout their years of
schooling so that they may make steady advancement and attain
the grades and diplomas which will enable them to achieve successfully in the next class or school and eventually in a working
role. In the slum school, however, teachers largely encounter pupils
who have not done well in their previous classes and are unable to
do well in their present ones. The formal curriculum is frequently
inappropriate for these pupils, and teachers find themselves engaged in initiating work activities which their students cannot do
at all or can only do poorly.

The experience of trying to implement a curriculum among
pupils for whom it has little meaning is a frustrating one. This
frustration may be increased by administrators who censure teachers for departures from the formal curriculum or fail to supply the
working conditions and educational tools and resources which
teachers believe would help their pupils do better work. Even those
teachers who do not initiate activities disturbing to administrators,
or who work under supervisors who are not disturbed by such activities, are likely to become frustrated by pupils who do not make
progress in the class. The discovery that not much is expected of
these students by other adults in the school may provide some relief
from this frustration. Nevertheless, the period of marking time until
one is assigned to a better class is often an agonizing one.

Experiences of failure are common among beginning teachers,
particularly among those who are unable to gain control of their
pupils in ways that satisfy themselves and administrators. Teachers
are expected to enforce bureaucratic rules and regulations and to
drill their pupils in the rituals of subordinate behavior which their
supervisors and usually they themselves believe to be necessary if
pupils are to learn. This task is often extremely time-consuming and
unrewarded by pupils who are strange to or reject the behavior
required by the school. The amount of time spent on disciplining
pupils often precludes teaching them, with the result that educational goals are abandoned in favor of custodial ones. This process
is complete when the new teachers adopt the educational ideology
prevalent among many of the older teachers and reject some or all
of their pupils as being unworthy of education.

The induction of new teachers into the school in ways which
inhibit or even prohibit the establishment of significant learning
processess in the classroom means that teachers are often rejected

by many of their pupils and their parents. True induction into the classroom can occur only when those who are clients reach out and claim the personal and professional efforts as acceptable and meaningful for them. In the slum school, this does not typically occur, for both parents and pupils have traditionally been classified as those who properly have no involvement in setting the goals of the classroom or of the educational system. Hence even those teachers who are accepted by their supervisors and other teachers in the slum school may find that their pupils reject them as having nothing to offer that is educationally valuable. In these cases the induction into teaching is false, and neither teachers nor their clients are truly incorporated into an educational system worthy of the name.

The present educational crisis in which teachers find themselves in relationship to the urban poor is not of their own making nor one which will be resolved easily. It reflects deep and increasing social separations in urban regions and a serious lag between the types of educational institutions needed and those now available. It is the purpose of this final chapter to give consideration to these matters and to point out the social dimensions which must be taken into account if the educational rites of passage intended to incorporate teachers into their professional role are to achieve their goal in slum areas.

THE URBAN SEPARATION

The problems encountered by teachers attempting to educate children of the urban slum are in part an expression of the greatly increased separation of peoples in an urban world. Unlike small towns, where the inhabitants are highly visible and stand in well-defined relationships to each other, in a large metropolitan area people of diverse social backgrounds usually encounter one another only in casual ways or in relatively impersonal work situations. Contemporary metropolitan regions are characterized by both residential and occupational patterns which severely limit one's experience with and knowledge of persons who are very dissimilar to oneself. Those who live in more or less socially homogeneous metropolitan neighborhoods and suburbs have little opportunity to acquire a sense of the metropolitan region as a whole or the interdependence of its' several components. If they become involved in government, education, health, or welfare, they often confine their interest to local problems, giving little thought to the consequences of local actions on adjacent suburbs or neighborhoods, let alone those that are more remote spatially.

In the occupational realm, large modern business corporations and service agencies of all kinds bring together a wide range of persons to perform the specialized functions required in a technological society. More often than not, these business and service organizations are oriented toward more than local concerns, and many are even international in scope. At the same time, the human organization within these establishments inhibits personal experience with the metropolitan population as a whole. There is first the organization of positions within firms and agencies on a graded basis, with specific specialized skills required for each position, and different rewards, responsibilities, and prestige provided to those who are at the varying levels. Interaction between those at different levels is usually within the context of supervision, in which conscious efforts are made to keep relationships impersonal and limited to the solution of work problems. Therefore, it is possible to share a place of work with those of divergent social class and cultural origins without learning much about them or their personal relationships and activities.

Secondly, the large work organizations each have a specialized function in our society, and often the training required to obtain a position in these organizations is so specialized that it precludes a general understanding of the society in which the training is to be utilized and prohibits exposure to those who are trained with different perspectives and understandings about the nature of the world. Intensive interaction with only those whose training is like one's own tends to create and maintain professional and technical enclaves which are culturally isolating and which inhibit the development of interdependent relationships and of a sense of the way one's work relates to the needs of the whole community.

The types of urban residential and occupational separation described above are mutually supportive of each other and substantially contribute to the difficulties encountered by contemporary teachers and others who work in slum areas. Usually coming from areas of the metropolis which are not inhabited by the poor, teachers have very little, if any, personal acquaintance with the values, customs, life circumstances, and social background of the pupils they meet in the slum school. The fact that the cultural backgrounds and perspectives of teachers and pupils are often widely divergent increases the potential for conflict which already exists in the classroom because of age and social class differences.

The distance, geographical and social, which separates teachers from their pupils is accompanied by professional training which has usually enshrouded teachers in social isolation as a result of their position in the educational system. When they begin their first teaching assignments, they are already committed to a definition of their professional role as those who impart their superior knowledge and technical skill to pupils within a bureaucratically organized educational system which stresses impersonal relationships. This very emphasis discourages the establishment of friendly relationships with pupils and the exchange of personal information in the classroom which might give teachers at least some insight into the pupil's world. The lack of any significant contacts with the community or the homes of their pupils shields teachers from a knowledge of the social environment within which their pupils spend most of their time. The potential for cross-cultural learnings and relationships through classroom activities is stifled by the rigidities of the formal curriculum and its modes of presentation which discourage the discovery of pupils' interests and the use of their experiences in the school. Teachers are isolated also from their superiors through their bureaucratic exclusion from the decision-making process concerning the way in which classroom work is to be planned and undertaken.

In support of the above tendencies, the professional training of teachers often prepares them to accept the present organizational structure of the educational system as "natural" and something that cannot be changed. It is, after all, the system in which many of them have been educated and which has proven successful for them and their teachers. By emphasizing techniques of education which are functional for the system and psychological interpretations of child behavior, the training tends to render teachers incapable of viewing themselves, their pupils, parents, school administrators, and the school itself within the context of the community and society in which education supposedly takes place. In this way the professional ideology transmitted in the training school may perpetuate the traditions of a bureaucratic approach to education in an urban world which demands other approaches if children are to be educated and not merely managed.

The professional training frequently adds further to the cultural isolation of the teachers by exposing them solely to American middle-class versions of the ways children "ought" to behave in school, even though it may furnish them with some experience of the ways children from other backgrounds do behave. Finally, since it does not give teachers a sense of the metropolitan region as a whole or of the flexibility necessary to the educational system if all are to be provided with opportunities to become incorporated into the new urban America, the professional training fails to enable teachers to make the transition into this society and leaves them as encapsulated within their own socio-cultural backgrounds as those whom they would try to teach.

TEACHING IN AN URBAN WORLD

The special crisis faced by teachers in slum areas as a consequence of the separation of people in the urban world which does not allow either pupils or teachers to experience the community as a whole is compounded by the tendency to make the teacher the scapegoat in the situation. Like nurses in hospitals, teachers are the most visible professional agents among the many employees of the organizations in which they work. The high visibility of teachers in contrast to the relative invisibility of administrators who determine the policies for the local school places them in an especially vulnerable position. It is the teacher who most often receives pupil complaints about the school and the brunt of pupil dissatisfaction, boredom, and hostility. Frequently too, parents who are unhappy with the school single out individual teachers or groups of teachers to attack. More subtly, but with extremely widespread consequences, the educational research concerned with classroom dynamics has focused on the teacher's personality, background, and behavior as an important variable in the classroom but has seldom considered the social situation within which the classroom is found or the teacher's lack of power in the educational system. Similarly, teacher training institutions and programs devote most of their work to attempts to mold and change the behavior of teachers but comparatively little effort to changing the educational system within which they work.

In view of the tendency of the teacher training institutions, the educational system, and those whom the school serves to single out teachers as those who must change if children are to be better educated, it is not surprising to discover that in most proposals for remedying the problems in the slum school the greatest attention has been given to teachers. In some proposals, emanating primarily from militant Negro leaders, it is suggested that many, if not all, of the present teachers in schools attended primarily by Negroes should be replaced by Negro teachers, who would presumably be better able to relate to Negro pupils. Other proposals stress the need for training programs for teachers who are already in service in these schools or about to be assigned to them, and the need to screen teachers more carefully before sending them into the slum school. Still other proposals stress the need for the recruitment of persons from the community, idealistic youth from other communities, or a greater number of more experienced teachers to serve in the slum school. Despite the merits which these proposals may contain, they fail to come to grips with the reorganization of the educational system demanded not only by the slum school but also by our times.

It is misleading to single out the teacher as the only, or even the most important, educational leader in the school. To do so is to revert to an image of the teacher which was true of the rural or small-town school but is no longer so in the complex educational system of metropolitan life. In fact, teachers in the contemporary school are so subordinate to those who coordinate, supervise, and manage their activities that they have had to become increasingly militant in unions and professional organizations to have any voice at all in matters of vital concern to them.

To teach in the urban world of today is to become an employee of a large educational bureaucracy in which the teaching-learning function of the school has tended to be replaced by that of management and custodial care. The present situation is the result of a historical development which began with the growth of student populations in urban areas in the mid-nineteenth century. As larger numbers of students were educated for longer periods of time, school systems increased in size, and more complex procedures were developed for classifying, grouping, and instructing pupils. These developments, in turn, led to the need for some uniformity of educational procedures and practices and to the establishment of administrative offices in the school system for the purpose of coordinating the work of teachers in the classroom and ensuring that pupils had equal opportunities to advance in the school system to the best of their ability. In recent times, teachers have been increasingly subordinated to a professional elite of administrators and specialists who occupy more prestigious positions in the school than they and largely determine the educational policies which they are to implement.

The displacement of educational goals by managerial ones is evident in many situations, but especially in the ceremonial events which mark the transition from the role of student to that of teacher. As those progressing from one group to another in a large-scale organization which makes fine distinctions between the occupants of different positions, new teachers participate in a number of special ceremonial events intended to facilitate their passage from the defined position of student to the equally defined position of teacher. These ceremonies are not dramatic, colorful events accompanied by pageantry, trumpetry, and solemnity intermingled with joy; rather, they are routine events of bureaucratic life, accompanied by official written memoranda, verbal directives, and often by apathy and boredom. In particular, they are the ceremonies of orientation to the school, the opening of school, supervisory classroom observation, and public display, by means of which supervisors attempt to train new teachers to conform to the orderly bureaucratic procedures which set the boundaries within which the work of teaching and learning is to be done and to prepare them for their role in the classroom.

Within the classroom, new teachers are trained to lead ceremonial activities which "routinize" the child for his position in the educational system. These ceremonies provide the means of symbolically acting out the teacher-pupil relationship believed to be necessary for the teaching of the curriculum prescribed by others far removed from the local school. Efforts are made to condition pupils to their non-management roles as workers who are to produce the work which the educational management deems necessary for advancement in the school system. The instructional relationship frequently resembles traditional industrial relations between foremen and workers. For Negro pupils especially, the relationship may be demeaning and perpetuate types of passive behavior which are no longer functional for them in the modern world.

Parental and student boycotts of schools in slum areas, the apathy and hostility of many children in these schools, and the poor morale among teachers and administrators are all symptoms of needed changes in the organizational structure within which parents, pupils, and educators must work. At present this is a structure which denies personal freedom and autonomy to individuals to solve their problems and forces them to serve the educational organization rather than placing it in the service of their needs. Cases in point are teachers who must arrange their schedules to fit the schedules of specialists, parents who must remain home from work if they are to confer with teachers, and pupils who must be socially adept if they are to be educated.

Teaching in the contemporary urban slum requires bridging the gap between the segregated world of the socially mobile professional educator and the segregated world of the poverty-stricken lay client. A transition into a role of significant educational leadership cannot be made by those who are deeply committed to and entrenched in the perpetuation of a model of the professional-client relationship which in city after city has proven itself bankrupt in meeting the educational needs of illiterate children. Considerably more than the traditional ritualized responses of an outdated bureaucracy are required if those children are to make the necessary transition into our society and if teachers are to find satisfaction and professional identity in teaching them.

What is required is nothing less than a reorganization of the school in such a manner that both teachers and pupils are restored to a central position and other functions of the school are made subsidiary to that of teaching and learning. Teachers are indeed the most crucial professional agents in the school, and pupils and their parents are the most important clients of the school. However, there is little in the current organization of schools which treats either teachers, pupils, or parents as persons of worth and dignity, capable of exercising initiative and making autonomous decisions about school policy.

Coming together from two quite different social worlds, teachers and pupils in the classroom of the slum area are assigned to roles which perpetuate and intensify the social distance between them. In the encounters which follow most pupils and teachers fail to achieve success and a sense of personal and social identity within the formal classroom group. Informally, teachers typically retreat into segregated colleague groups, and pupils retreat into equally segregated groups of peers. They each view the educational system from their own vantage point, and there is little exchange of views or opportunity to systematically work together on common problems within either the formal or informal system of relationships in the school. The business of running the school is not considered the task of pupils and teachers in any event, but is delegated to administrators and, to a lesser extent, to specialists and selected teachers who have administrative responsibilities in addition to their other duties. Parents are supposed to help the school but are perceived as intruders if they attempt to make decisions about matters of school policy. Similar to teachers, they can only make their views known by joining pressure groups which are capable of voicing sufficient protest to effect changes. Pupils also must employ highly visible means of social protest if they are to make their positions known, and at least some of the outbursts of vandalism, assault, and obscenity in slum schools need to be viewed as attempts on the part of students to express, in the only ways they know, feelings of deep dissatisfaction with the educational system.

The crisis in slum schools will not be resolved simply by placing different teachers or more teachers in these schools, shifting a given proportion of pupils to other schools, introducing isolated experimental programs, increasing police protection, or even providing the money for more goods and services. At best these approaches represent piecemeal attempts whose effectiveness is likely to be lost within the present organizational structure. Such changes can only be effective if they occur within school systems flexible enough to respond to the continually changing needs of pupils and to actively solicit the aid of outsiders from the community and the metropolitan region in finding solutions to problems of common concern. Unfortunately educators have often not had training which prepares them to understand the social nature of the problems with which they must cope. Equally unfortunate is the fact that many in other fields who are in a position to help are not familiar with the problems of educators, especially in slum areas. Urgently needed is a new organization combining human and technological resources in both the teacher training centers and the schools which can incorporate a diversity of persons, including teachers, pupils, and parents, to work out solutions to common problems in local situations.

The question is no longer whether or not resources are available to greatly improve the situation. In an affluent technological America, they surely are. What is still uncertain is the extent to which the resources will be utilized imaginatively in the difficult task of creating schools in which the children of the poor and those who teach them are incorporated into significant roles in our society. The alternative is schools as we now know them in which many pupils and teachers merely serve time until they can drop out into their respective metropolitan enclaves. From this perspective, the crisis faced by teachers in slum schools is one shared by all Americans, for the educational system reflects our society. Pupils will either be prepared to participate significantly in the schools and in society or be abandoned by them.

APPENDIX A

Data Collection

The primary sources of data used in this book are the weekly tape-recorded reports of thirteen beginning elementary-school and nine beginning junior-high-school teachers who told of their experiences in public schools in slum areas over a period of time which began on the Saturday prior to the opening of school and continued throughout early January. For the former group, the time span was Saturday, September 7, 1963 through Saturday, January 11, 1964. The junior-high-school teachers reported a year later, beginning on Saturday, September 12, 1964 and concluding on Saturday, January 8, 1965.

The teachers returned each week to the college from which they had graduated. They reported fifteen times each on consecutive Saturdays, with the exception of Saturdays which fell within major holiday periods. Teachers who had to miss a Saturday session because of illness or other personal reasons made their reports at other times during the week.

With two exceptions, all of the reports were made individually. The elementary-school teachers made their reports on recording equipment in the language laboratory of the college. The junior-high-school teachers used tape recorders located in the audio-visual department of the college. Because this equipment was not accessible on the first Saturday that the elementary-school teachers were to report, they were divided into two groups for group recordings under the direction of the project staff. A similar problem on November 14, 1964 resulted in a group session on that date for the junior-high-school teachers. While the usual procedure was for the teachers to come to the college to record on Saturday mornings, one of the junior-high-school teachers recorded at home and mailed in a weekly tape, and a second junior-high-school teacher regularly recorded on a weekday. In both cases, there were special circumstances which made these arrangements necessary.

A total of sixty-four primary questions were asked of the elementary-school teachers during the fifteen recording sessions. All except three of these questions were repeated for the junior-high-school teachers, who were asked a total of seventy-five primary questions, including fourteen questions which had not been used among the elementary-school teachers. Typically, a primary question included one or more secondary questions designed to elicit more detailed reports from the teachers about the area of primary concern. Among the questions used in both groups, three questions were used at each of the fourteen sessions following the opening of school. Two questions were asked at thirteen sessions; two questions were repeated at twelve sessions and one question was asked on four occasions. The remainder of the questions were asked only once.

The number of primary questions asked at any one session ranged from six to fourteen for the elementary-school teachers and from six to sixteen for the junior-high-school teachers. The questions were rexographed, and in nearly all cases the teachers were given or mailed the questions in advance of the recording session.

The order in which the questions appeared remained the same over time. Questions 1, 4, 5, 2, and 3, listed below, were presented in that order, beginning at the third session. The next week, questions 6 and 7 were added as regular weekly questions. On the four weeks when it was asked, question 8 was placed between questions 6 and 7. The non-recurring questions (9-78) were added to the above basic set of questions, in the order in which they appear in the following list.

Although some questions were identical for both groups of teachers, others had to be edited so as to take into account the greater complexity of the junior-high school and the fact that teachers in these schools teach several different classes. The complete list of questions used, the number of times each was asked, and the date on which it appeared are given below.

During the week following each recording session, members of the project staff and several members of the faculty in the teacher education program at the college each listened to one or two of the reports given by the teachers. Each teacher was assigned to one of these listeners who responded to the teacher in a letter and asked him or her a limited number of additional questions to clarify what had been said. The purpose of this listening procedure, however, was primarily to enable the teachers to feel that someone was genuinely interested in their reports and to provide a human response to the material. The individual letters and questions were given to each teacher on the next Saturday and answered at that time. The listeners were trained to refrain from evaluative comments and questions and the giving of advice. While the individual questions yielded some additional material, this was minimal in contrast to that already provided by the responses to the following questions given to everyone:

LIST OF QUESTIONS ASKED AT RECORDING SESSIONS

Questions Asked at Fourteen Sessions

Elementary-School Teachers (September 14, 1963 through January 11, 1964):
Junior-High-School Teachers (September 19, 1964 through January 8, 1965):

1. What is the most important thing that happened to you in your school this week? Describe this event in detail. What were your feelings when this happened?

*2. Describe in detail your interaction with the administrative staff of the school this week. In so far as you can, tell when and where the interaction took place. Who was involved in the interaction, and who initiated the interaction? For each event that you describe tell as fully as you can what was involved in the interaction.

*3. Describe in detail your interaction with other teachers in the school this week. In so far as you can, tell when and where the interaction took place and who initiated the interaction. With what teacher (or teachers) have you had the most interaction? What have you learned from other teachers? What things have you discussed with other teachers this week?

Questions Asked at Thirteen Sessions

Elementary-School Teachers (September 21, 1963 through January 11, 1964):
Junior-High-School Teachers (September 16, 1964 through January 8, 1965):

4. Describe your most successful lesson during the past week. Tell what

*As noted earlier, several of the questions asked of the elementary-school teachers were slightly edited so as to make them applicable to the junior-high-school situation. These questions are preceded by an asterisk in the following list. Although the revised questions are not presented, they may be obtained from the author.

materials you used. Give an outline of what you attempted to do. How did the children react? Why did you feel this particular lesson was more successful than others you undertook?

*5. Describe your least successful lesson during the past week. Tell what materials you used. Give an outline of what you attempted to do. How did the children react? Why did you feel this particular lesson was less successful than others you undertook?

Questions Asked at Twelve Sessions

Elementary-School Teachers (October 5, 1963 through January 11, 1964):
Junior-High-School Teachers (October 3, 1964 through January 8, 1965):

*6. Describe the two or three children with whom you had the most difficulty during the past week. Had you had difficulty with these children before? What did you do to handle those children who were difficult? What do you plan to do about the problem in the future?

*7. Have any children been transferred in or out of your class since September 20th (for example, during the past two weeks)? If so, why were they transferred? What class are they now in (or what class did they come from)? Who decided they should be placed in or removed from your class? How did you feel about these changes in the class? [The date given in this question was changed from week to week.]

Question Asked at Four Sessions

Elementary-School Teachers (October 5 and 12; December 7 and 14, 1963):
Junior-High-School Teachers (October 3 and 10; December 5 and 12, 1964):

*8. Describe the two or three children with whom you had the least difficulty during the past week. How is their behavior different from that of the most difficult children?

Questions Asked at One Session

Junior-High-School Teachers   (September 12, 1964):

9. Please tell us in which school you did your student teaching. In which subject area and in which grade or grades was your student teaching experience? Did you participate in Project_____? Have you worked as a substitute teacher? If so, please tell us in which school, in which subject area, and in which grade was your substitute teaching experience.

Elementary-School Teachers (September 7, 1963):
Junior-High-School Teachers (September 12, 1964):

*10. Please tell us in what school you are teaching and what class you will
be teaching. Was this school your first, second, or third choice? Why
did you choose this particular school in which to teach? (Or if you did
not choose the school but were assigned to it, please tell us how you
feel about the assignment.) On the basis of what you know about the
school so far, what are your expectations of what teaching will be like
in this school? If this school was not your first choice, what school (or
schools) would you have preferred?

Elementary-School Teachers (September 7, 1963):
Junior-High-School Teachers (September 12, 1964):

*11. Please tell us about the formal meetings you have attended this week.
What did you learn about the school and your class at these meetings?
Who spoke at the meetings and what formal printed, audio-visual, etc.
materials were used at the meetings? In addition to the formal meetings you attended, what did you learn about the school and your class
informally? (For example from informal talks with teachers and others,
your own observations, etc.)

Elementary-School Teachers (September 7, 1963):
Junior-High-School Teachers (September 12, 1964):

*12. What did you know about the school and your class prior to attending
the meetings this week? From what sources did you learn these
things? Did what you learned this week confirm or change your expectations of what the school and your class is like? In what ways
were your expectations confirmed or changed? In what ways do you
think this school is similar to and/or different from the school in which
you did your practice teaching?

Elementary-School Teachers (September 7, 1963):

13. What, if any, discussion was there of the potential teachers' strike at
the meetings you attended this week? How does the strike threat
affect you as a beginning teacher? Have you been approached to participate in the strike? If you have, what response do you plan to make?

Elementary-School Teachers (September 7, 1963):
Junior-High-School Teachers (September 12, 1964):

*14. What, if any, discussion was there of the potential boycott of the
schools at the meetings you attended this week? How does the threat
of the boycott affect you as a beginning teacher?

Elementary-School Teachers (September 7, 1963):
Junior-High-School Teachers (September 12, 1964):

*15. What do you plan to do at the first session of your class on this coming Monday?

Elementary-School Teachers (September 14, 1963):
Junior-High-School Teachers (September 19, 1964):

*16. Tell about your first day in class. What was it like? What happened that you had expected? What unexpected things happened? What was the best thing that happened on your first day? What was the worst thing that happened? How did you feel about teaching at the end of the first day? About the school? About the children?

Elementary-School Teachers (September 14, 1963):
Junior-High-School Teachers (September 19, 1964):

*17. What are your impressions of your class after the first week of school? What problems (if any) do you think you will have in teaching them? Did you anticipate these problems or are they ones you had not thought of before? What things (if any) have you been told about your class in general and specific individuals in the class? By whom have you been told these things? Do you agree or disagree with what you were told?

Junior-High-School Teachers (September 19, 1964):

18. Describe the classes with which you expect to have the least difficulty and the classes with which you expect to have the most difficulty.

Elementary-School Teachers (September 14, 1963):
Junior-High-School Teachers (September 19, 1964):

*19. Describe the two or three children with whom you expect to have the least difficulty and the two or three children with whom you expect to have the most difficulty. What is there about these children that leads you to think they will or will not present difficulties to you? How do you plan to handle the children you think will be difficult? Have you had any real discipline problems so far? If so, what did you do about them? [The reader will note the similarity between this question and questions 6 and 8. After the first two weeks this question was divided into two questions and rephrased.]

Elementary-School Teachers (September 14, 1963):
Junior-High-School Teachers (September 19, 1964):

*20. After your first week as a teacher, how do you feel about your job?
What things have you enjoyed most this week? What things have you
least enjoyed? What thing (or things) do you plan to really stress with
your class by the end of the week? What had you expected to accomplish this week that you were unable to accomplish?

Junior-High-School Teachers (September 19, 1964):

21. What effect (if any) did the boycott have on your school? On your
class? How do you think the boycott will affect your school in the
future?

Elementary-School Teachers (September 21, 1963):
Junior-High-School Teachers (September 26, 1964):

*22. Describe your class as it existed on Friday, September 20th. How
many are in the register? How many boys are there? How many girls
are there? In so far as you can tell, what is the socio-economic background of the children? What is the ethnic background? What is the
range of reading scores, arithmetic scores, and I.Q. scores of the children in your class? Have any children been transferred out of your
class during the past two weeks? If so, why were they transferred and
what class are they now in? Who decided they should be transferred?
How did you feel about the transfer of these children out of your
class? Have you had any new children enter the class during the past
two weeks? If so, why were they transferred into your class? Who
decided they should be placed in your class? How did you feel about
these new children entering your class?

Elementary-School Teachers (September 21, 1963):
Junior-High-School Teachers (September 26, 1964):

*23. What textbooks are being used in your class? Do you have copies of
these books for each child? Have you started using them? Do you feel
that these books will be useful to you in your teaching? Why?

Junior-High-School Teachers (September 26, 1964):

24. Last week you described the classes with which you expected to have
the most difficulty and those with which you expected to have the
least difficulty. Do you still feel the same way about these? After your
second week of teaching, would you make any changes in those you
expected to be the most or least difficult? Why?

Elementary-School Teachers (September 21, 1963):
Junior-High-School Teachers (September 26, 1964):

25. Last week you described the two or three children with whom you expected to have the most difficulty and those with whom you expected to have the least difficulty. Do you still feel the same way about these children? After your second week of teaching, would you make any changes in those you expected to be the most or least difficult? Why?

Junior-High-School Teachers (September 26, 1964):

26. Are you required to submit a plan book? Have you been given any instructions concerning its preparation? By whom?

Junior-High-School Teachers (October 3, 1964):

27. Can you describe the greatest difference between being a teacher and being a student teacher? For example, impressions of the school, the administration, relations with teachers and children, supervision of your work, your conduct and emotions in the classroom, your feelings about the job, etc. Are there any similarities that strike you as being important?

Elementary-School Teachers (October 12, 1963):
Junior-High-School Teachers (October 10, 1964):

*28. As of October 11, 1963, what supplies and/or textbooks are lacking in your class? Do you have everything you need? Have you received everything you have requested? How have you managed without books or supplies (if you have had to do so)? What is the procedure for requesting texts or supplies in your school? With what ease or difficulty are you able to obtain books and supplies?

Elementary-School Teachers (October 19, 1963):

29. Are you keeping an anecdotal record about any of your children? If so, for which children are you keeping the record? Why are you keeping records on these children? How will you use the record?

Elementary-School Teachers (October 19, 1963):
Junior-High-School Teachers (October 17, 1964):

*30. Give us as complete a description of your school building as you can. Be sure to include such items as the following: the location of the school, the year it was built, the modernization the school has had in recent years (if any), any special features of the physical layout (such as annex). In describing your building assume that we have never seen it. First describe the outside. Then take us through the building floor by floor, giving us the location of classes, offices, lunchrooms, etc., by floor. Where is your room in relation to the rest of the build- ing? Other classrooms? Administrative offices? The lunchroom? The pupils' cafeteria? What physical features of your building are an asset in teaching? A liability? If you could change the building, what im- provement would you make? If you would find it easier to bring in a floor plan of your building rather than to describe it, feel free to do so.

Elementary-School Teachers (October 19, 1963):
Junior-High-School Teachers (October 17, 1964):

*31. How many classes are there on your grade level? What is the range of exponents? What is the significance of the exponent in your school? (For example, does a low exponent mean a bright class and a high exponent a low class, or is there a different system?)

Elementary-School Teachers (October 26, 1963):
Junior-High-School Teachers (October 24, 1964):

*32. Give us as complete a description of your classroom as you can. Be sure to include such items as the following: location of your class- room; approximate size; shape; classroom furnishings (n.b. do you have movable chairs and tables or are they fixed to the floor?); gen- eral appearance of room; use of wall space (for example, how much wall space is used for windows, blackboards, cupboards, etc.?). What problems does your room present to you as a teacher? In what ways is teaching aided or hindered by the room you are in? If you could change the room, what changes would you make?

Elementary-School-Teachers (October 26, 1963):
Junior-High-School Teachers (October 24, 1964):

33. Have you been asked for a copy of your plan book by any of the administrators? If so, how often have you been requested to turn it in? Who looks at your plan book? What is her or his position in the school? What comments have been made about your plan book? Have you consulted with other teachers about plan books? With whom have you talked and what have they advised? How often do you have to turn in your plan book?

34. Describe the assembly program for your class. Who participates in them? Have you led any of them or do you expect to? What is the purpose of the assembly program for your grade level? Has your class (or individuals in it) received any special awards or commenda- tions at assembly? If so, please describe.

Junior-High-School Teachers (October 31, 1964):

35. Have any of your pupils asked questions or made statements that surprised you? Please describe them.

Elementary-School Teachers (November 2, 1963):
Junior-High-School Teachers (October 31, 1964):

36. Have you been observed as yet by anyone from the administrative staff of the school? If so, when and by whom were you observed? Were you given advance notice that you would be observed? If so, what effect did this have on your lesson? What was said, if anything, to you by the observer after he had completed the observation?

37. Give us as complete a description of the neighborhood surrounding your school as you can. Be sure to mention if your school is in the midst of a housing project or if there are any other outstanding features about the immediate environs. Do you have any fear about working in this neighborhood? If so, why? Do you take any special precautions in this neighborhood? Have you been given any special directions about precautions that need to be taken?

Junior-High-School Teachers (October 31, 1964):

38. Have you received copies of the Board of Education publications_____and_____? Please describe in detail how you received them. Have there been any discussions in school by administrators or teachers concerning these pamphlets? Have you read them? Do you believe they will have any influence upon your teaching?

Elementary-School Teachers (November 9, 1963):
Junior-High-School Teachers (November 7, 1964):

*39. In so far as you can, describe the informal groupings of teachers within your school. How many definite cliques or subgroups have you been able to distinguish? Who is in each of these groups? What common characteristics, if any, do the members of each subgroup have? (For example teach the same grade, all of one sex, graduates of the same school, etc.) What would you say are the most common attitudes about teaching, the schools, and related matters of the different subgroups?

Elementary-School Teachers (November 9, 1963):
Junior-High-School Teachers (November 7, 1964):

40. Have you yourself become part of a definite subgroup in the school? With whom do you regularly share common activities of a formal

nature? With whom do you regularly share common activities of an informal nature? For each of the above groups (those with whom you share formal activities and those with whom you share informal activities), describe the shared activities in detail. Describe as fully as you can (for those in each group) the attitudes toward teaching, the school, and related matters of each of the others.

Elementary-School Teachers (November 9, 1963):
Junior-High-School Teachers (November 7, 1964):

*41. Describe as fully as you can the system of rewards and punishments which you have found to exist in your school. What types of discipline are used in the school? How is good behavior rewarded? Have you been under any special pressure to adopt one or more forms of discipline as contrasted with others? Is corporal punishment ever used in your school? If so, when? Who administers it?

Elementary-School Teachers (November 9, 1963):
Junior-High-School Teachers (November 7, 1964):

42. What are the procedures in your school for seeing parents? Have any parents come in to see you about their children? Which ones? Are parents free to come any time? Do you make appointments with them? Does the principal arrange for parent visits? Have there been any meetings of the Parents' Association? Who attended from the school? Have there been any other formal meetings involving parents? Did you attend? If so, which parents did you meet? Tell us about any meetings you have attended which involved parents. Also please tell us in detail any experiences you have had with parents since the beginning of the year (it is not necessary to repeat material you have already taped).

43. Is the arrangement of your room (bulletin boards, use of wall space, exhibits, books, arrangement of furniture, etc.) largely a matter which you decide and over which you have control? Or are there special requirements? How did you learn about them? What pressure, if any, have you been under to have displays, etc.?

Elementary-School Teachers (November 16, 1963):
Junior-High-School Teachers (November 14, 1964):

44. Have you recently been asked to fill out a form telling the racial distribution of children in your class and the language spoken by the children? If you have this data available, it would be helpful to us if you could give us the data.

45. How many holdovers do you have in your class? For each holdover that you have, will you please tell us his or her name, how many times

he or she has been held back, and the number of years he or she was held back on each occasion.

46. Please list the names, authors, and publishers of the textbooks and workbooks you are using in your class. Do you find these textbooks and workbooks adequate for your class? Are they too advanced or too easy for your group or do you find them about right? What has led you to this conclusion? If you could write or change the textbooks and workbooks, what changes would you make?

47. What textbooks, workbooks, and other supplies do you feel you need for your class that you do not now have? What (if any) seems to be the difficulty in obtaining these? What have you done to try to obtain needed books or supplies? Have your efforts been successful? What adaptations have you had to make in your teaching as a result of lack of books or supplies?

Junior-High-School Teachers (November 14, 1964):

48. Have any of your pupils said things or done things which have surprised you? If so, please tell us what happened and why you were surprised?

Elementary-School Teachers (November 23, 1963):
Junior-High-School Teachers (November 21, 1964):

49. In addition to the administrative and teaching staff of your school, what interaction have you had with other school personnel? (For example teacher aides, custodial staff, clerical and secretarial staff, etc.) In so far as you can, try to give us a summary of this interaction over the past several weeks using the questions under 4 and 5 as a guide.

Elementary-School Teachers (November 23, 1963):
Junior-High-School Teachers (November 21, 1964):

*50. What kinds of groupings (if any) are you using in your class? When do you use groups? To what extent do you find them helpful or harmful in teaching? Please give us a summary of the ways in which you organize classroom work for each of the several subject areas? How do you supervise the work of the children and find out how well they are doing? (For example do the children hand in written work, do you check the work of children at their desks, etc.?) In what ways (if any) do you reward good work and/or attempt to improve poor work?

Elementary-School Teachers (November 23, 1963):
Junior-High-School Teachers (November 21, 1964):

51. What problems do you have planning lessons for your classes? What

difficulties (if any) do you have in finding appropriate materials for your lessons? Making transitions between lessons or within a given lesson? Providing for individual or group differences in the class?

To what extent does the plan book you turn in represent the work you are actually able to accomplish in class? In what subject areas (if any) is there apt to be a discrepancy between what you plan to do and what you are actually able to do? What do you feel to be some of the reasons for this discrepancy?

Have any of the children in your classes brought you presents or shown other signs of affection (for example compliments, kissing)? How do you feel about these? To what extent do they present a problem to you?

Junior-High-School Teachers (November 21, 1964):

52. Did parents visit any of your classes this week? How did you feel about having them there? Did you prepare a special lesson for their visit? How did the children behave? Please describe anything concerning the parents' visit you feel would be of interest.

Elementary-School Teachers (December 7, 1963):
Junior-High-School Teachers (December 5, 1964):

53. Have you prepared any special materials for use in your class (for example, rexographed materials)? How did you happen to prepare these materials? Have they been useful? *Would you please bring in an extra copy of any materials you have especially prepared (provided you have a copy you can spare) and let us have it for our files?* Do you enjoy preparing these kinds of materials?

54. Have you had or do you plan to have any contacts with others who may be working with any of the children in your class but who are not connected with the school (for example, community leaders such as social workers, psychiatrists, scout leaders, settlement house workers, clergymen, etc.)? If you have not already done so, will you please tell us about these contacts? Who initiated them? Where did they occur? What happened as a result?

Elementary-School Teachers (December 7, 1963):
Junior-High-School Teachers (December 5, 1964):

*55. Now that you have been teaching for three months, how do you feel about your job? What things have you enjoyed the most? What things have you least enjoyed? What things had you hoped to accomplish with your class by this time that you have been able to accomplish? Unable to accomplish? What has facilitated or hindered the accomplishment of these things?

Elementary-School Teachers (December 7, 1963):
Junior-High-School Teachers (December 5, 1964):

56. As of this date, do you plan to teach next year? What school do you hope to teach in? *If you plan to teach in the school where you are now located,* what class would you like to have? (Please specify grade level and the level within the grade.) Have you made any preliminary moves to try to get this class? How have you gone about it? Do you think you will get this class? Why? *If you plan to teach in a different school,* please tell us what school you hope to teach in. (Please specify the exact school if you know and the type of school it is—also please specify the grade level and the level within the grade that you would like to teach in this school.) Have you made any preliminary moves to try to get a job in this school? How have you gone about it? Do you think you will get a position there? Why? Do you think you will be teaching the class of your choice? Why? *If you don't plan to teach next year, what are your plans?*

57. So far, what is the best thing that has happened to you in your teaching career? Describe the event and how you feel about it. What is the worst thing that has happened to you? Describe the event and how you feel about it. What are the things that have happened that you had expected? What are the things that have happened that you had not expected?

Elementary-School Teachers (December 7, 1963):
Junior-High-School Teachers (December 5, 1964):

*58. How do you feel about teaching? About your class? About the school? Do you ever secretly wish that you had not gone into teaching or had a different class or were in a different school? If so, what would you rather do? What class do you wish you had? What school do you wish you were in? Have you encouraged any of your friends to teach in your school? Why? Have you ever thought about doing substitute teaching rather than regular teaching? Why?

Junior-High-School Teachers (December 12, 1964):

59. Please describe in detail your homework assignments for this week. Why did you choose to give these assignments? What is your procedure concerning the assignment of homework? (For example, beginning of period, end, during the lesson; mimeographed, dictated, blackboard.) How did you arrive at this procedure? How often do you assign homework? Are there times when you assign extra homework or less homework? Do you assign the same homework to all the classes of the same grade? Describe any method of follow-up or checking and grading of homework you do. What problems, if any, do some children seem to have with homework?

60. Do you require your pupils to keep a notebook? If so, please describe in detail any instructions you gave the children concerning the note-book. Do you have a procedure for checking or marking? If so, please tell us about your procedures and criteria for marking. Describe the characteristics of the notebooks you have seen.

Junior-High-School Teachers (December 19, 1964):

61. Please tell us in as much detail as possible what factors you believe to be involved in your children's success or failure in school. How do you measure success or failure? How do you believe the children can be helped to be more successful?

62. Does your school have any Special Progress classes? If so, do you know how these classes are formed? Have these classes remained intact or have there been children transferred in or out of them?

Elementary-School Teachers (January 4, 1964):
Junior-High-School Teachers (January 8, 1965):

63. Did you do anything special for or with your class in connection with Christmas? If you did, will you please describe what you did and how the children reacted?

64. Since you began teaching, how many times have you been absent? How many times have you been late? What is the policy in your school for handling absences or tardiness?

65. Are there any teachers in your school that you would hold up as models of good teaching? Who are they? What (if anything) have you learned from them? What qualities do these teachers have that make you feel they are good models of teaching?

66. Are there any teachers in your school that you would hold up as models of poor teaching? Who are they? What (if anything) have you learned from them? What qualities do these teachers have that make you feel they are poor models of teaching?

Elementary-School Teachers (January 4, 1964):
Junior-High-School Teachers (January 8, 1965):

*67. Do you know anything about any other public elementary schools in _____other than the one you work in? How do other schools compare with your school? Is there any school you know about that you would hold up as a model of a good school? A poor school? Why? If you were describing your school to a friend, would you describe it as a good school? A poor school? Why?

Elementary-School Teachers (January 4, 1964):
Junior-High-School Teachers (January 8, 1965):

68. Have you recently had to fill out report cards for your class? What problems (if any) did this present to you? Who are the five children in your class who received the best report? Who are the five children who received the poorest report? For each child you name, summarize briefly the report you made about him or her.

Elementary-School Teachers (January 4, 1964):
Junior-High-School Teachers (January 8, 1965):

*69. Please describe a typical school day. In doing your description, please give the details of how your day starts, the regular events that happen (for example the morning exercises), the time of the day that various things occur, etc.

Junior-High-School Teachers (January 8, 1965):

70. What help have you had in curriculum planning? How often do you meet as a group to work on effective methods of teaching? What have you done on your own to increase your knowledge of subject matter and to learn more about planning classroom experiences. (If you are teaching out of license, tell what you have done in this area as well as your own subject area.)
71. Have you participated in any professional organizations, attended any meetings outside your own school? Do you view teaching as a challenge and as an interesting experience, which will inspire you to progress in the profession?

Elementary-School Teachers (January 11, 1964):

72. Since the first week in November (the last time we inquired about this) have any parents come to see you about their children? Which ones? Have you made any home visits? Which homes did you visit? Have there been any meetings of the Parents' Association? Did you attend? If so, which parents did you meet? Tell us about any meetings you have attended which involved parents. Also please tell us about any experiences you have had with parents that you have not already described on previous tapes.

Elementary-School Teachers (January 11, 1964):
Junior-High-School Teachers (December 19, 1964):

73. Tell us about the work activities that you are currently sharing or doing together with other teachers and administrators in the school.

For each activity you describe, please tell us the names of the persons with whom you work.

74. Tell us about the non-work activities you are currently sharing or doing together with other teachers and administrators in the school. For each activity you describe, please tell us the names of the persons with whom you share these activities. (Be sure to include such groups as your lunch group, any group or persons you see after school, etc.)

Elementary-School Teachers (January 11, 1964):
Junior-High-School Teachers (December 19, 1964):

*75. Please tell us in as much detail as possible what the current profile of your class is. What is the range of reading scores? Are there any children for whom you feel the score as officially recorded by the school is inaccurate or misleading? (For example, are there children who read better or worse than you had anticipated on the basis of their scores?) If you have not clearly done so in the past, please tell us the racial distribution in your class and the percentage of children on welfare in your class. What is the age range? If any of the children are older or younger than one would normally find at your grade level, would you please let us know which ones they are and (if you know) how they happen to be in your class.

Elementary-School Teachers (January 11, 1964):

76. How do you feel about the threatened boycott of the school in February? If there is a boycott, how do you think it will affect your school? Your class? Yourself? Have you discussed the boycott with any of the other teachers? Are there any Negro or Puerto Rican teachers in your school? Have you talked about the boycott with them? How do they feel? How do other teachers feel?

Elementary-School Teachers (January 11, 1964):
Junior-High-School Teachers (December 19, 1964):

77. What is the current number of children in your class? How many boys are there? How many girls? Out of this number, how many children do you feel are keeping up with the amount and kind of work that you perceive as desirable for your class? How many are behind in their work but making sufficient progress for you to feel that they are among the working members of your class? How many are so far behind that you feel they cannot participate meaningfully in classroom work? Are there any children in your class who you feel really belong in another class? Which children? Why do you feel they should be elsewhere? Where should they be?

Elementary-School Teachers (January 11, 1964):

78. What influence (if any) do you think participating in this project (the Saturday taping sessions) has had on your experiences as a beginning teacher? Do you think it has influenced your teaching in any way? How?

In addition to the teachers' reports, two other sources of data were used. The student teaching and other college records of each teacher were consulted to provide background data with respect to grade averages, the evaluation of the teacher by student teaching supervisors, and employment during the college years. Paper and pencil questionnaires were given to the teachers as a means of readily gathering information on such matters as their socio-economic background, past and current formal education, and characteristics of the schools in which they taught, and, in the case of the elementary-school teachers, the length of time they estimated that they spent on various classroom ativities. These questionnaires were given to the teachers at the recording sessions, but were completed by them during the week and returned. At the end of the school year, each teacher was mailed a questionnaire requesting information about plans for teaching the following year, and the school and classes in which they would be located.

Characteristics of Classes Taught by Twenty-two Teachers*

ELEMENTARY-SCHOOL TEACHERS

1. **Ruth Abraham:** Fourth-grade class in School G. Out of seven fourth-grade classes in this school, this class ranked third in ability and achievement. Between September and January the enrollment ranged from 28 to 29. Approximately half were boys and half were girls. Two-thirds of the pupils were Puerto Ricans, all of whom spoke English. One-third of the pupils were Negroes. Seventy-five per cent of the pupils' families were on welfare. All of the pupils had I.Q. scores under 100. Although all of the pupils were supposed to be reading on the third-grade level, in January 1964 one read at the first-grade level, one at the second-grade level, and a few at fourth- and fifth-grade levels. On a mathematics achievement test given to the class in October, most of the pupils scored in the 10th percentile, and some scored in the 20th and zero percentiles. There were five holdovers in the class.

2. **Claire Altman:** Sixth-grade class in School I. Out of five sixth-grade classes in this school, this class ranked the lowest in ability and achievement. Between September and mid-November, the enrollment ranged from 28 to 22. Slightly less than two-thirds were boys, and slightly more than a third were girls. In November, 77 per cent of the children were Puerto Ricans, half of whom had been born in Puerto Rico. The remainder of the children were Negro. Five of the Puerto Rican pupils spoke English as well as could be expected of those their age; the remainder used a good deal of "idiomatic Spanish." Most of the pupils' families were on welfare. The range of I.Q. scores was 66 to 133, but only two pupils had scores of 85 or better. The range of reading ability was 3.1 to 4.2. On a mathematics achievement test, one pupil scored at the 40th percentile, eighteen scored at the 80th percentile, one at the 20th percentile, and two at the 10th percentile. There were fifteen holdovers in the class.

3. **Helen Bauer:** First-grade class in School I. Out of five first-grade classes

*All names of teachers and schools are pseudonyms. Additional information about the characteristics of these teachers and schools is given in Appendixes C and D.

that met in a split session in the afternoon, this class ranked the lowest. Between September and January the enrollment ranged from 25 to 27. Approximately half were boys and half were girls. There were three Negroes in the class. The remainder of the children were Puerto Rican. The socio-economic status of the pupils is unknown, and due to their grade level, there is no information on I.Q. or mathematics scores. Most of the pupils had not attended kindergarten. Only six of the pupils spoke English well. The others did not speak English at all or spoke it with an accent. On a reading readiness test, one pupil scored at the 80th percentile, one at the 60th percentile, five at the 50th percentile, and four at the zero percentile. The scores of the other pupils are unknown. Since this was a first-grade class, there were no holdovers.

4. **Hilda Conway:** Third-grade class in School D. Out of five third-grade classes in this school, this class ranked fourth in ability and achievement. Between September and mid-November, the enrollment ranged from 26 to 33. After a reorganization of third-grade classes in the school in early October, two-thirds of the pupils were boys, and one-third were girls. About half of the pupils were Negro and half were Puerto Rican. Approximately half of the pupils' families were on welfare. The range of I.Q. scores was 85 to 118. In November, the reading scores ranged from 1.5 to 3.2, but most of the class was approximately two years retarded in reading. No information is available on the range of mathematics scores. There were seven holdovers in this class.

5. **Myra Delehanty:** Second-grade class in School J. Out of ten second-grade classes in this school, this class ranked fourth in ability and achievement. Between September and January, the enrollment ranged from 30 to 29. Half were boys and half were girls. Slightly more than a quarter of the pupils were Puerto Ricans, none of whom were born in Puerto Rico and all of whom spoke English well. The remainder of the pupils were Negroes. With one exception, all of the pupils' families were on welfare. The range of I.Q. scores was 90 to 123. Most pupils read at the 1.1 level. On a mathematics achievement test, only one pupil scored at the 99th percentile. The rest of the class scored below the first-grade level. There were two holdovers in the class.

6. **Florence Ferber:** Fourth-grade class in School D. Out of seven fourth-grade classes in this school, this class ranked second in ability and achievement. Between September and January, the enrollment ranged from 35 to 28. Slightly more than a third of the class were boys, and slightly less than two-thirds were girls. Approximately 60 per cent of the class were Puerto Ricans, about half of whom were born in Puerto Rico and none of whom spoke fluent English. Forty per cent of the pupils were Negroes. Between 60 and 75 per cent of the pupils' families were on welfare. The range of I.Q. scores was 70 to 100. About a third of the class read at the 3.0 to 3.5 level. On a mathematics achievement test, one pupil scored at the 40th percentile, most pupils

scored between the 10th and 20th percentiles, and four pupils scored at the zero percentile. The number of holdovers in the class is unknown.

7. **Hannah Gimbel:** Second-grade class in School C. Out of five second-grade classes, this class ranked third in ability and achievement. Between September and November, the enrollment ranged from 30 to 28. Half were boys and half were girls. Two of the pupils were Puerto Ricans who had been born in the United States and who spoke English. The remaining pupils were Negroes. Seventy-five to ninety per cent of the pupils' families were on welfare. The range of I.Q. scores was 75 to 100. The majority of pupils were reading at the 1.4 to 1.6 level. Two pupils were reading at approximately the second-grade level, and five read at pre-primer level. On a mathematics achievement test, the majority of pupils scored at the 10th or 20th percentile. There were two holdovers in the class.

8. **Rose Giordano:** Third-grade class in School A. Out of two third-grade classes in this school, this class ranked second in ability and achievement. Between September and November, the enrollment was 31. Approximately two-thirds were boys and one-third were girls. Three of the children were Negroes. Twenty-five were Puerto Ricans, of whom all but one had difficulty speaking English. Three pupils were from other ethnic backgrounds. Most of the pupils' families were on welfare. The range of I.Q. scores is unknown. Thirteen pupils read at the 1.0 level, thirteen at the 1.2 level, four at the 1.3 level, and one on the third grade level. The level of mathematics achievement is unknown. There were approximately ten holdovers in this class.

9. **Arlene Goldsmith:** Fifth-grade class in School B. Out of four fifth-grade classes in this school, this class ranked second in ability and achievement. Between September and January, the enrollment ranged from 34 to 35. Approximately 60 per cent were girls and 40 per cent were boys. The majority of pupils were Puerto Rican, only one of whom could not speak English. There were a few Negroes in the class. The socio-economic status of the pupils was low, but no information is available on the number of pupils whose families were on welfare. One pupil had an I.Q. score of 66. The range of I.Q. scores for the rest of the pupils was 85 to 111. The range of reading scores was 2.8 to 4.2, and four of the pupils read above the fourth-grade level. On a mathematics achievement test, the range of scores was from the zero to the 30th percentile. There were three holdovers in the class.

10. **Jean Levine:** Third-grade class in School J. Out of ten third-grade classes in this school, this class ranked fifth in ability and achievement. Between September and January, the enrollment ranged from 29 to 28. Slightly more than half the class were boys, and slightly less than half were girls. Two-thirds of the class were Negroes. One-third were Puerto Ricans. Only one child was born in Puerto Rico. Six or seven of the Puerto Rican pupils were bilingual and spoke English well. The

majority of the pupils' families were on welfare. One pupil had an I.Q. score of 65, and one had a score in the high 90's. Most I.Q. scores were in the high 70's or low 80's. Most of the pupils read on the first- or second-grade level and were on the third-grade level in mathematics. There were two holdovers in the class.

11. **Deborah Schultz:** Fifth-grade class in School E. Out of four fifth-grade classes in this school, this class ranked second in ability and achievement. Between September and January, the enrollment ranged from 29 to 25. Approximately two-thirds of the class were girls, and one-third were boys. There were three Negroes in the class. Seventeen of the pupils were Puerto Ricans, only one of whom was born in Puerto Rico, and only two of whom had difficulty with English. The rest of the pupils were from other ethnic backgrounds. The majority of the pupils' families were on welfare. The range of I.Q. scores was 73 to 116, and the median I.Q. score was 93. In January all of the pupils read at the fourth- or fifth-grade level, although at the beginning of the school year most were reading at the high third-grade and the fourth-grade level. On a mathematics achievement test most of the class scored at the 40th or 50th percentile. The range was from the zero to the 90th percentile. There were seven holdovers in the class.

12. **Eleanor Stein:** Fourth-grade class in School F. Out of four fourth-grade classes in this school, this class ranked second in ability and achievement. Between September and January the enrollment ranged from 29 to 33. Slightly less than 60 per cent of the pupils were girls, and slightly more than 40 per cent were boys. Slightly less than a third were Negroes, and the remainder were Puerto Ricans. Of the Puerto Ricans, three spoke English fluently; most spoke with an accent but could communicate well; only one had considerable difficulty with speaking English. The socio-economic status of the pupils' families was low, but the number on welfare is unknown. The majority of I.Q. scores were in the high 80's; one score was 115. The range of reading scores was 2.2 to 3.2. Scores on mathematics tests are not known but were stated to be low. There were five holdovers in the class.

13. **Frances Wood:** Second-grade class in School H. Out of eight second-grade classes in this school, this class ranked sixth in ability and achievement. Between September and January, the enrollment ranged from 27 to 22. Approximately half were boys and half were girls. Five of the pupils were Negro, and the remainder were Puerto Ricans. All of the Puerto Rican pupils spoke some English, and four of them spoke English well. The majority, however, had varying degrees of difficulty with English. Approximately 60 per cent of the pupils' families were on welfare. One child had an I.Q. score of 111. A third of the class had scores in the mid 70's. The remaining scores were not available. Six of the pupils read at the primer level, five

were non-readers, and the rest were reading at the pre-primer level. On a mathematics achievement test, the range of scores was from zero to approximately the 35th percentile. There were three holdovers in the class.

JUNIOR-HIGH-SCHOOL TEACHERS

14. **Carol Bretton:** Taught English to one seventh-grade and two eighth-grade classes in School O. All of her teaching was in license. Her official class comprised 25 seventh-grade pupils, almost equally divided between boys and girls, and Negroes and Puerto Ricans. Their I.Q. scores ranged from 85 to 103. Their ability range in reading was 3.3 to 4.6, and in mathematics it was 3.0 to 4.2.

The two eighth-grade classes were as follows: (1) A class composed of 33 pupils, in which there were twenty-two boys and eleven girls. The class was approximately evenly divided between Negroes and Puerto Ricans. The range of reading scores was 3.8 to 6.0, and mathematics scores ranged from 4.2 to 6.1. (2) A class composed of 28 pupils, evenly divided between boys and girls and Negroes and Puerto Ricans. The range of reading scores was 4.0 to 9.2, and mathematics scores ranged from 4.0 to 6.3.

15. **Edith Cramer:** Taught English to one seventh-grade class and two eighth-grade classes and social studies to one seventh-grade class in School L. Her teaching in English was out of license. Her official class, to which she taught social studies, comprised 35 seventh-grade pupils, of whom fourteen were girls and twenty-one were boys. The class was largely Puerto Rican and Negro. Three of the pupils were from other ethnic backgrounds. The range of reading scores was from 3.7 to 4.9, and mathematics scores ranged from 4.3 to 7.0.

The seventh-grade class, to which she taught English, comprised 41 pupils, nearly evenly divided between boys and girls. The majority were Negroes and Puerto Ricans, but two pupils were from other ethnic backgrounds. The range of reading scores was 4.2 to 5.9 and mathematics scores ranged from 4.4 to 7.0.

The two eighth-grade classes to which she also taught English were as follows: (1) A class composed of 33 pupils almost evenly divided between boys and girls. Four of the pupils were from other ethnic backgrounds, but the remainder were Puerto Ricans and Negroes. In mathematics and reading the pupils were two to three years below grade level. (2) A class composed of 38 pupils, almost evenly divided between boys and girls. Eight of the pupils were from other ethnic backgrounds, but the remainder were Puerto Ricans and Negroes. In mathematics and reading the pupils were one year or less below grade level.

16. **Frank Gibbs:** Taught social studies to four ninth-grade classes in School

Q. All of his teaching was in license. He did not have an official class. The ninth-grade classes were as follows: (1) A class composed of 27 pupils, of whom ten were boys and seventeen were girls. Three were Negroes, two were Puerto Ricans, and twenty-two were from other ethnic backgrounds. In reading their scores ranged from 9.1 to 12.7, and their mathematics scores ranged from 6.7 to 12.8. (2) A class composed of 35 pupils, of whom thirteen were boys and twenty-two were girls. Five were Negroes, two were Puerto Ricans, and twenty-eight were from other ethnic backgrounds. In reading, their scores ranged from 9.2 to 12.1, and in mathematics their scores ranged from 6.1 to 11.0. (3) A class composed of 30 pupils, of whom seventeen were boys and thirteen were girls. Nine were Negroes, one was Puerto Rican, and twenty were from other ethnic backgrounds. In reading their scores ranged from 6.2 to 11.9, and in mathematics they ranged from 5.2 to 10.0. (4) A class composed of 13 pupils, of whom seven were boys and six were girls. Seven were Negroes, and six were from other ethnic backgrounds. In reading their scores ranged from 4.2 to 5.8, and in mathematics they ranged from 2.8 to 6.1.

17. **Martha Grant:** A *per diem* substitute who had no official class or regular subject classes. Some of her substitute work was out of license, and some was in license (social studies). As a substitute she taught a range of grades, subjects, and ability groups in School M.

18. **Rachel Lawson:** Taught English to three seventh-grade classes in School P. All of her teaching was in license, and all of her classes comprised girls only. Her official class had an enrollment of 27, of whom all were Negroes except for one Puerto Rican. Their I.Q. scores ranged from 80 to 90, and in reading and mathematics their ability ranged from the third- to the fifth-grade level.

    The two other classes were as follows: (1) A class comprising 32 pupils, of whom all were Negroes except for two Puerto Ricans. Their I.Q. scores ranged from 90 to 110, and in reading and mathematics their ability ranged from the fourth- to the sixth-grade level. (2) A class comprising 26 pupils, all of whom were Negroes. Their I.Q. scores ranged from 85 to 95, and in reading and mathematics their ability ranged from the third- to the fifth-grade level.

19. **Sarah Marsh:** Taught English to one seventh-grade and two eighth-grade classes in School P. All of her teaching was in license. Her official class comprised 34 eighth-grade pupils, of whom twenty-two were boys and twelve were girls. All were Negroes. Their reading scores ranged from 3.6 to 8.6, and their mathematics scores were not given.

    The two other classes were as follows: (1) An eighth-grade class composed of 33 pupils, of whom fifteen were boys and eighteen were girls. All were Negroes. Their reading scores ranged from 3.8 to 7.1, and their mathematics scores were not given. (2) A seventh-grade class, composed of 26 boys. Twenty-four were Negroes, one was Puerto Rican, and one was from another ethnic background. Their reading scores ranged from 3.2 to 4.6, and their mathematics scores were not given.

20. **Julius Rosenblum:** Taught English to two eighth-grade classes and two seventh-grade classes in School L. All of his teaching was out of license. His official class comprised 27 pupils in the seventh grade, of whom sixteen were boys and eleven were girls. Eleven were Puerto Ricans, fifteen were Negroes, and one was from another ethnic background. The range of reading scores was 3.5 to 3.9, and the range of mathematics scores was 3.9 to 6.5.

The three other classes to whom he taught English were as follows: (1) A "very bright" seventh-grade class composed of 37 pupils, of whom twenty-two were boys and fifteen were girls. The majority were Negroes. The next largest ethnic group was Puerto Rican. There were a few in the class from other ethnic backgrounds. Reading and mathematics scores were not given, but presumably this class was on or above grade level. (2) A "slow" eighth-grade class composed of 25 pupils, of whom fourteen were boys and eleven were girls. About 50 per cent of the class were Negroes, and 50 per cent were Puerto Ricans. Reading and mathematics scores were not given. (3) A "very bright" eighth-grade class composed of 40 pupils, of whom fifteen were boys and twenty-five were girls. Nearly all were Negroes, although a few were Puerto Ricans and several other ethnic backgrounds were represented. The reading and mathematics scores were not given.

21. **Alice Stern:** Taught mathematics to four seventh-grade classes and remedial reading to one eighth-grade class in School K. All of her teaching was out of license. Her official class, to whom she taught mathematics, was the bottom class in the seventh grade. The enrollment was 26 for most of the term, about evenly divided between boys and girls. Six pupils were Negro, eighteen were Puerto Rican, and two were from other ethnic backgrounds. The range of reading scores was from non-readers to 3.3, and mathematical ability was at the fourth-grade level or below. The pupils all understood English but did not speak it grammatically. There were several holdovers in this class.

The three other seventh-grade classes to which she taught mathematics were as follows: (1) A top talent class composed of 32 pupils, of whom thirteen were boys and nineteen were girls. Twelve were Negroes, fourteen were Puerto Ricans, and six were from other ethnic backgrounds. In reading and mathematics all of the pupils were on the seventh-grade level or above. (2) A talent class composed of 30 pupils, of whom eighteen were boys and twelve were girls. Eleven were Negroes, seventeen were Puerto Ricans, and two were from other ethnic backgrounds. The range of reading ability was from fifth to seventh grade. In mathematics, the range was from sixth to seventh grade. (3) An average class composed of 30 pupils about evenly divided between boys and girls. This class was mostly Puerto Rican and

Negro. Most read on grade level, but some were only at the fifth-grade level. In mathematics, the class was at the fifth- to the seventh-grade level.

The eighth-grade class to which she taught remedial reading was composed of eleven pupils, of whom five were boys and six were girls. Two were Negroes and nine were Puerto Ricans. In reading and mathematics their work was at the fourth- to the sixth-grade level.

22. **Margaret Wiener:** Taught English to one ninth-grade and three seventh-grade classes in School N. All of her teaching was in license. Her official class was composed of 36 ninth-graders, of whom fifteen were boys and twenty-one were girls. Eight were Negroes and twenty-seven were Puerto Ricans. One pupil came from a different ethnic background. She did not teach her official class. The four classes to whom she did teach English were as follows: (1) A ninth-grade class composed of 35 pupils, of whom fifteen were boys and twenty were girls. (2) A seventh-grade class composed of 36 pupils who were a "little behind to average" in ability. (3) A seventh-grade class which was "a little above average." (4) A seventh-grade class composed of 35 pupils who were "slow." No further information is given about the characteristics of these four classes.

APPENDIX C

Characteristics of Schools to Which Teachers Were Assigned

			Ethnic Distribution			
School	Enrollment	Year Built	%Negro	%Puerto Rican	%Other	No. of Asst. Principals

A. ELEMENTARY SCHOOLS

School	Enrollment	Year Built	%Negro	%Puerto Rican	%Other	No. of Asst. Principals
A	540	1895	10	60	30	0
B	850	1921	34	65	1	1
C	900	1903	98	2	–	1
D	1000	1954	50	50	–	1
E	1000	1957	10	80	10	1
F	1035	1900	48	51	1	2
G	1200	1959	18	78	4	2
H	1400	1891	22	74	4	2
I	1430	1957	22	74	4	3
J	1500	1896°° 1962	85	15	–	3

B. JUNIOR HIGH SCHOOLS

School	Enrollment	Year Built	%Negro	%Puerto Rican	%Other	No. of Asst. Principals
K	1000	1950	25	50	25	3
L	1200	1962	45	35	20	4
M	1225	1955	50	50	–	4
N	1300	1935	15	65	20	3
O	1700	1910	45	55	–	5
P	1900	1896°° 1942	98	2	–	7
Q	?	1930's	25	3	72	3

° Part-time, usually one to three days a week.
°° Schools J and P each had an old annex which was used in addition to the main building which was constructed later.

			Number of Specialists			
Reading	Speech	Non-English	Teacher Training	Guidance	Music	Science
1°	1°	1°	–	1	–	–
1-1/2	1°	–	1°	1	–	–
1	1°	–	–	2	1	–
2	1°	–	–	1	–	1
1-2/5	1°	1	–	1°	–	1
3	1°	1	–	2	–	1
2	1°	1	1°	1	–	–
2	–	1	1°	1	1	–
1-3/5	1°	1	1°	1°	1	1
3	1°	2	–	3	1	–
?	1°	1	–	2	–	–
2-1/5	1°	–	–	2	–	–
3-1/5	1°	1	1	4	1	1
2-2/5	1°	1	–	2	1	1
2-1/5	1°	–	–	4	–	–
4	1°	–	1	6	–	1°
–	1°	–	–	1	–	–

Socio-economic Characteristics of Twenty-two Teachers*

ELEMENTARY-SCHOOL TEACHERS

1. **Ruth Abraham:** Female. White. Jewish. Age 22. Born in U.S.A. Engaged and living with parents. Graduate of local public elementary and secondary schools. Father born in U.S.A.: mother born outside of U.S.A. Father completed college and attended graduate school. Mother completed high school. Father employed as post-office foreman. Mother employed in photographic business. Family income is between $9,000 and $9,999. Two people contribute to this income, and four people are supported by it.

2. **Claire Altman:** Female. White. Jewish. Age 20. Born in U.S.A. Single and living with mother. Graduate of local public elementary and secondary schools. Both parents born in U.S.A. Father completed high school. Mother attended but did not complete elementary school. Father deceased. Mother unemployed. Family income is between $5,000 and $5,999. One person contributes to this income, and three people are supported by it.

3. **Helen Bauer:** Female. White. Jewish. Age 21. Born in U.S.A. Married and living in own household. Graduate of local public elementary and secondary schools. Both parents born in U.S.A. Both parents completed high school. Father employed as a cutter. Mother unemployed. Family income is between $8,000 and $8,999. One person contributes to this income, and six people are supported by it.

4. **Hilda Conway:** Female. White. Catholic. Age 21. Born in U.S.A. Single and living with mother. Graduate of local parochial elementary and secondary schools. Both parents born outside of U.S.A. Father completed high school. Mother completed elementary school. Father deceased. Mother employed as dressmaker. Family income is between $6,000 and $6,999. One person contributes to this income, and three people are supported by it.

5. **Myra Delehanty:** Female. White. Catholic. Age 22. Born in U.S.A. Engaged and living with parents. Graduate of local parochial elementary and secondary schools. Father born outside of U.S.A.; mother born in

*All names are pseudonyms.

158

U.S.A. Both parents completed high school. Father employed as foreman. Mother unemployed. Family income is between $8,000 and $8,999. One person contributes to this income, and three people are supported by it.

6. **Florence Farber:** Female. White. Jewish. Age 20. Born in U.S.A. Engaged and living with parents. Graduate of local public elementary and secondary schools. Both parents born in U.S.A. Father completed college. Mother completed high school. Father employed as pharmacist. Mother employed as secretary. Family income is unknown.

7. **Hannah Gimbel:** Female. White. Jewish. Age 21. Born in U.S.A. Married and living in own household. Graduate of local public elementary and secondary schools. Both parents born outside of U.S.A. Both parents attended but did not complete high school. Father employed in garment industry. Mother unemployed. Family income is between $8,000 and $8,999. One person contributes to this income, and two people are supported by it.

8. **Rose Giordano:** Female. White. Catholic. Age 21. Born in U.S.A. Engaged and living with parents. Graduate of local parochial elementary and secondary schools. Both parents born in U.S.A. Both parents completed high school. Father employed as postal clerk. Mother employed as clerk. Family income is between $6,000 and $6,999. Two people contribute to this income, and five people are supported by it.

9. **Arlene Goldsmith:** Female. White. Jewish. Age 21. Born in U.S.A. Married and living in own household. Graduate of local public elementary and secondary schools. Both parents born in U.S.A. Father attended but did not complete high school. Mother completed high school. Father employed as a school custodian. Mother employed as a typist. Family income exceeds $15,000. Three people contribute to this income, and five people are supported by it.

10. **Jean Levine:** Female. White. Jewish. Age 20. Born in U.S.A. Single and living with parents. Graduate of local public elementary and secondary schools. Both parents completed college. Mother also did graduate work. Father employed as a certified public accountant. Mother employed as a teacher. Family income is between $10,000 and $14,999. Two people contribute to this income, and five people are supported by it.

11 **Deborah Schultz:** Female. White. Jewish. Age 20. Born in U.S.A. Single and living with parents. Graduate of local public elementary and secondary schools. Both parents born in U.S.A. Father attended but did not complete college. Mother completed college. Father employed as salesman. Mother unemployed. Family income is between $10,000 and $14,999. One person contributes to this income, and four people are supported by it.

12. **Eleanor Stein:** Female. White. Jewish. Age 22. Born in U.S.A. Single and living with parents. Graduate of local public elementary and secondary schools. Both parents born in U.S.A. Father attended graduate

school. Mother completed college. Father employed as pharmaceutical detailman. Mother employed by the city. Family income is between $10,000 and $14,999. Two people contribute to this income, and four people are supported by it.

13. **Frances Wood:** Female. White. Catholic. Age 22. Born in U.S.A. Single and living with parents. Graduate of local parochial elementary and secondary schools. Both parents born in U.S.A. Father completed high school. Mother attended but did not complete college. Father employed as traffic manager. Mother employed as bacteriologist. Family income is between $6,000 and $6,999. Two people contribute to this income, and two people are supported by it.

JUNIOR-HIGH-SCHOOL TEACHERS

14. **Carol Bretton:** Female. White. Jewish. Age 21. Born in U.S.A. Engaged and living with parents. Graduate of local public elementary and secondary schools. Both parents born in U.S.A. Father attended but did not complete college. Mother completed high school. Father employed as window trimmer. Mother employed as medical secretary. Family income is between $5,000 and $5,999. Two people contribute to this income, and two people are supported by it.

15. **Edith Cramer:** Female. White. Jewish. Age 21. Born in U.S.A. Engaged and living with parents. Graduate of local public elementary and secondary schools. Father born in U.S.A.; mother born outside of U.S.A. Father attended but did not complete college. Mother attended but did not complete high school. Father employed as manager in textile firm. Mother employed part-time as bookkeeper. Family income is between $10,000 and $14,999. Two people contribute to this income, and three people are supported by it.

16. **Frank Gibbs:** Male. White. Protestant. Age 21. Born in U.S.A. Engaged and living with parents. Graduate of local public elementary and secondary schools. Father born outside of U.S.A.; mother born in U.S.A. Both father and mother attended but did not complete high school. Father employed as plant manager. Mother employed part-time as office worker. Family income is more than $15,000. No data available on how many contribute to this income, but three people are supported by it.

17. **Martha Grant:** Female. Negro. Protestant. Age 22. Born in U.S.A. Married and living in own household. Graduate of local public elementary and secondary schools. Both parents born in U.S.A. Father attended but did not complete college. Mother completed high school. Father deceased. Mother unemployed. Family income is between $3,000 and $3,999. One person contributes to this income, and three people are supported by it.

18. **Rachel Lawson:** Female. White. Religion unknown. Age: mid to late

twenties. Birthplace unknown. Married and living in own household. One child. Graduate of suburban public elementary and secondary schools. Completed part of college work in out-of-state public college. Birthplace, education, and occupation of parents and family income are unknown.

19. **Sarah Marsh:** Female. White. Catholic. Age 21. Born in U.S.A. Single and living with parents. Graduate of local parochial elementary and secondary schools. Both parents born in U.S.A. Father attended but did not complete college. Mother attended but did not complete high school. Father employed as office manager. Mother employed as a temporary comptometer operator. Family income is between $8,000 and $8,999. Three people contribute to this income, and four people are supported by it.

20. **Julius Rosenblum:** Male. White. Jewish. Age 22. Born in U.S.A. Single and living with parents. Graduate of local public elementary and secondary schools. Father born in U.S.A.; mother born outside of U.S.A. Father attended but did not complete elementary school. Mother completed high school. Father employed as a weather stripper. Mother employed as a school crossing guard. Family income is between $8,000 and $8,999. Two people contribute to this income, and five people are supported by it.

21. **Alice Stern:** Female. White. Jewish. Age 22. Born in U.S.A. Engaged and living with mother. Graduate of local public elementary and secondary schools. Both parents born in U.S.A. Both parents completed high school. Father deceased. Mother unemployed. No information available on family income.

22. **Margaret Wiener:** Female. White. Jewish. Age 22. Born in U.S.A. Single and living alone. Graduate of local public elementary and secondary schools. Both parents born in U.S.A. Father attended elementary school, but it is not known whether he completed elementary school. Mother completed high school. Father's occupation unknown. Mother employed as steno-typist. Family income is between $5,000 and $5,999. No information given on how many contribute to and are supported by this income.

Complaints of Elementary-School Teachers about Pupils in Their Classes

This tabulation is based on the 157 children described as "most difficult" and 56 additional children specifically mentioned as causing problems. Numbers in brackets refer to the number of children about whom the complaint was made.

A. Child engages in antisocial actions by
    1. Violating norms for classroom decorum and dress by
      a. Acting silly [4]
      b. Making faces and other gestures [6]
      c. Chewing gum [7]
      d. Mimicking others [5]
      e. Fidgeting [14]
      f. Leaving school books at home [13]
      g. Dressing improperly [8]
      h. Talking out of turn or shouting [41]
      i. Talking or whispering to self or neighbor [87]
      j. Passing notes [2]
      k. Singing, whistling, humming, or laughing [30]
    2. Violating spatial boundaries of classroom by
      a. Running or wandering around out of seat [52]
      b. Getting out of line [7]
      c. Leaving the room [26]
    3. Physically attacking other children by
      a. Engaging in fights [40]
      b. Hitting, pushing, kicking, or tripping them [48]
      c. Spitting at them [2]

4. Teasing, annoying, or picking on other children [32]
5. Verbally attacking teacher by
   a. Talking back, making disrespectful comments [31]
   b. Using obscene language [11]
6. Disobeying or disregarding teacher's orders [45]
7. Using objects inappropriately by
   a. Flinging them or knocking them over (for example, chairs) [5]
   b. Tearing or throwing them away (for example, papers and notebooks) [7]
   c. Banging, hitting, or stamping on them [6]
   d. Breaking and destroying school property [15]
8. Playing
   a. Disruptively by shooting and throwing things to others [13]
   b. Non-disruptively and independently [38]
9. Lying and stealing [23]
10. Not returning required notes and papers signed by parents [9]
11. Being tardy [17]
12. Being truant [13]
13. Generally misbehaving by making a fuss, acting up, fooling around [73]

B. Child has undesirable roles and relationships in the classroom because he or she is
   1. An instigator [9]
   2. A leader of a misbehaving group [1]
   3. A member of a misbehaving group [11]
   4. A scapegoat or reject [6]
   5. An isolate [5]
   6. A "show off" or clown [8]
   7. A ring leader [5]
   8. A tattletale [5]
   9. A flirt [3]
   10. A bully [3]
   11. Prejudiced [1]
   12. Engaged in an undesirable relationship (for example, antagonistic or too friendly) with another child [29]

C. Child gives evidence of a social-psychological problem:
   1. Withdrawn or shy [12]
   2. Fearful [5]
   3. Cries [20]
   4. Unhappy, depressed [5]
   5. Aggressive [8]
   6. Hostile [8]
   7. Obstinate or stubborn [8]
   8. Insolent, disrespectful, arrogant [13]
   9. Nervous [4]
   10. Hysterical [6]

11. Inconsistent [11]
12. Immature, babyish [25]
13. Emotionally disturbed [16]
14. Negative [3]
15. Other [16]
D. Child has poor scholastic achievement because of
  1. Academic handicaps due to
    a. Inability to speak English or other cultural differences [19]
    b. Lack of ability [32]
    c. Frequent absences [9]
    d. Underachievement [16]
  2. Low participation or lack of effort due to
    a. Active refusal to do schoolwork [26]
    b. Passive non-participation because of shyness or inability [12]
    c. Daydreaming or inattentiveness [46]
    d. Poor or careless work habits [27]
    e. Laziness [7]
    f. Lack of interest in learning [28]
  3. Inability to work by himself and need for constant attention [6]
  4. Not doing homework [31]
  5. Cheating, copying from others [4]
  6. Other reasons not mentioned above [18]
E. Child has health problems
  1. Visual deficiency [4]
  2. Dental caries [2]
  3. Fatigue [5]
  4. Hearing deficiency [1]
  5. Dizziness [1]
  6. Incontinent [3]
  7. Brain damaged [1]
  8. Infections [2]
  9. Speech impediment or difficulty [5]
 10. Other [3]
F. Child is poorly groomed or dressed [6]